PORSCHE
911E 911T 911S 911 2.7RS

ISBN 978-1-84155-637-6

CONTENTS

Porsche 911, Road Research Report, 1968	4
Porsche 911S, Road Test, Autocar, 1967	10
Porsche Type 911, Motor Sport, 1968	16
Porsche 911S, Road Test, Car & Driver, 1966	20
Porsche 911S, Driving Impressions, 1967	25
Porsche 911S, Sporting Motorist, 1967	26
Porsche 911S, Road Test, Road & Track, 1967	30
The New Porsches, Road & Track, 1969	34
1972 Porsche 911S, Motor Sport, 1972	35
Porsche 911E, Road Test, Road & Track, 1972	36
Porsche 911E, Sportomatic, Country Life, 1969	39
Porsche 911E, Road Test, Road & Track, 1971	40
Porsche 911 Sportomatic, Car & Driver, 1970	43
Porsche 911 Technical Data	48
Porsche 911S 2.2, Road & Track, 1974	54
Porsche Lineup, Road & Track, 1969	57
Porsche 911T Sportomatic, Road & Track, 1969	58
Porsche 911 Carrera 2.7 RS Touring, Autotest	62
Porsche 911T	68
Porsche 911S 2.7	71
Porsche 911S 2.7 Targa	74
Porsche 911E, Salon Feature, Practical Classics	78

Road Research Report:

PORSCHE 911

A new generation of Porsches proves they still have the master's touch . . . and then some

No contest. This is the Porsche to end all Porsches—or, rather, to start a whole new generation of Porsches. Porsche's new 911 model is unquestionably the finest Porsche ever built. More than that, it's one of the best *Gran Turismo* cars in the world, certainly among the top three or four.

Porsche enthusiasts used to insist that the 356 model was as nearly-perfect an automobile as had ever been designed, an immutable classic that couldn't be improved upon. Oh, no? Put a familiar 356 up alongside a 911. Only yesterday, the 356 seemed ahead of its time. Today you realize its time has passed; the 356 leaves you utterly unimpressed and you can't keep your eyes off the 911. The 911 is a superior car in every respect . . . the stuff legends are made of.

Let it be understood at the outset that the 911 does not replace the 356, according to the factory. In the catalog, it replaces the fussy, little-appreciated Carrera 2 while the 356C (ex-Super) and 356SC (ex-Super 95) still roll off the assembly lines at about their normal rate. However, we can't believe that Porsche will continue making two entirely different cars, side-by-side, beyond the immediately foreseeable future. And let it also be understood that the 911 is not readily available. The first six month's production is completely sold out and there's a line of expectant owners going halfway around almost every Porsche agency in the country.

GENERAL

The 911—so-called because it is the 911th design project since Porsche opened its doors in 1931—is also the first all-Porsche Porsche. The 356 was the first car to carry the Porsche name, although when it was conceived in 1948 it was little more than a souped-up, special-bodied version of an earlier Porsche design, the Volkswagen. The 911, while true to the 356's basic configuration, is an entirely new and different car. The engine is again air-cooled, again hung out behind the rear axle, but it's a single-overhead-cam six-cylinder where the 356 was a pushrod four-cylinder (and the Carrera a four-cam four-cylinder). The new body is far more handsome—the work of old Professor Porsche's grandson, Ferry, Jr. The 911's 5-speed gearbox, already in service in Porsche's 904 GT racing car, is probably the new car's best single feature. Even the suspension is new, though tried-and-true torsion bars are retained as the springing medium.

The 911, or 901 as it then was, was introduced at the 1963 Frankfurt Auto Show. It was very much a prototype and its debut may have been premature. More than a year was to pass before it went into production, during which time the model number was changed (to indicate that it was a later model than the Frankfurt car and also because Peugeot reportedly had a lock on three-digit model numbers with zero in the middle), the price estimate dropped, the performance estimate rose, and a demand built up that the current four-a-day supply won't be able to satisfy for some time to come.

The 901/911 was not the "best" car Porsche could have made. Porsche could have put the storied flat-eight engine into production, bored out to, say, 2.5 liters and tuned up to 240 horsepower. That would have put the 901/911 into the Ferrari-Corvette-Jaguar performance bracket. It also would have raised the price considerably, and Porsche was understandably nervous about entering the No-Man's-Land market for $9000 GT cars. On price alone, it would have been beyond the reach of anybody but the Very Rich, and the V.R. are noted for such capricious perversity as preferring a $14,000 car to a $9000 car simply because it costs $5000 *more*. The four-cam flat-eight also would have had the same kind of maintenance and reliability problems the Carrera engine had; problems that are hopefully nonexistent in the 911's sohc six-cylinder.

Considering what the Stuttgart design office has turned out in the past, Porsche *could* have come out with a supercharged six-liter 550-hp V-16 GT car to sell for $30,000 and not lose a drag race to anybody but Don Garlits, but their production facilities are hardly geared for that sort of thing, and it would be getting pretty far away from the Porsche image, wouldn't it? In fact, Porsche had a full four-seater on the drawing boards at one point, but Ferry Porsche felt that his company's business was not selling super-duper sedans or ultra-ultra sports/racing cars but optimum-priced, optimum-size, optimum-performance *Gran Turismo* cars, which is exactly what the 911 is.

At $6490 POE East Coast (or $5275 FOB Stuttgart), the 911 isn't what you'd call cheap—no Porsche ever was—but then, quality never is. Porsche's kind of quality cannot be had for less, viz. Ferrari 330GT ($14,000) or Mercedes-Benz 230SL ($8000). It's of more than ordinary interest that the 911 costs a whopping thousand dollars *less* than the Carrera 2 it replaces. A Porsche is either worth it to the prospective buyer or it isn't; he can't justify the price tag by the way the body tucks under at the rear or by the way the steering wheel fits in his hands or the way the engine settles in for a drive through a rain-filled afternoon. But let's see what he gets for his money.

BODY

The 911's eye-catching body is distinctive—slimmer, trimmer, yet obviously Porsche. While not as revolutionary as the original 356 design was in its day, the 911's shape is far less controversial and slightly more aerodynamic. Though frontal area has grown, a lower drag coefficient (.38 vs. .398) allows it to reach a top speed of 130 mph on only 148 hp. It ought to weather the years without looking dated. Compared to the current 356 body, the 911 is five inches longer (on a four-inch longer wheelbase), three inches narrower (on a one-inch wider track) and just about the same height. The body structure is still unitized, built up of innumerable, complicated steel stampings welded together (with the exception of the front fenders which are now bolted on for easier repair of minor accidents). The glass area and luggage space have been increased 58% and 186%, respectively, and the turning circle is a bit tighter. The fully-trimmed (with cocoa mats) trunk will hold enough for a week's vacation for two; additional space is available in the rear seat area. The trunk and engine lids can be opened to any angle and held by counter-springs and telescopic dampers—a nice touch. These lids, as well as the doors, are larger than the old Porsche's, making access to the innards much less awkward. The gas filler cap nestles under a trap-door in the left fender, and the engine lid release is hidden away in the left door post.

The generous expanse of glass area does wonders for the rearward vision; all-around visibility is comparable to a normal front-engined car. The bumpers are well-integrated with the body, though provide barely adequate protection from those who park by ear. The standard appointments are lush and extensive: two heater/defrosters, padded sun-visors with vanity mirror, map and courtesy lights, 3-speed windshield wipers, 4-nozzle windshield washers, chrome wheels, belted tires, two fog lamps, a back-up light and a beautiful wood-rim steering wheel. About the only options we'd like are seat belts (for which massive, forged eyebolts are provided), a radio and a fender mirror. Fitted luggage and factory-installed air-conditioning will be available shortly, we're told.

INTERIOR

The ads tell you a Porsche is "fun" to drive. Fun? A Mini-Minor is fun to drive because it can't be serious; everything about it is incongruous—it defies all known laws of nature . . . and marketing . . . and gets away with it. The Porsche—*any* Porsche—is no fun at all; Germans aren't much given to frivolity. Porsches are designed by drivers, for drivers, to be driven very matter-of-factly from Point A to Point B in maximum comfort, speed and safety. Form soberly follows function, and the cockpit of a Porsche is laid out to achieve just that end. The controls and instruments are efficiently positioned, and this economy of effort and motion is why Porsches aren't tiring to drive. But *fun?* Porsches are for *driving*.

As befits a driver's car, the controls are superb. The steering wheel is a special joy; the shallow "X" of the black anodized spokes provides perfect thumbrests without obscuring any of the unusually comprehensive instrumentation. The reach to the wheel is just right, and all the secondary controls are operated by stalks on either side of the wheel. The driver can signal for turns; flash, raise and dip the headlights; and operate the windshield wipers and washers, all without moving his hands from the wheel. The gearshift lever has less travel than the 356's, is smoother and requires no more effort. The pedals are beautifully positioned for long-distance touring or fancy heel-and-toe footwork; there's even room to rest the left foot between the clutch and the front wheel arch.

The seats have the wondrously-comfortable Reutter reclining mechanisms, and are softly sprung and upholstered in cloth with leather edges. They will adjust to fit anybody under seven feet and 300 pounds. Head- and hip-room are similarly commodious; shoulder room is about the same as in the 356. The rear seats are a different matter. Though the 911 is occasionally described as a 2+2, the space back there is *very* cramped. It can hold an adult—sitting sideways with head bent forward—or a child, but neither for very long. It is more properly a luggage area, and for that purpose the seat backs fold down to form a shelf for a couple of fair-sized suitcases.

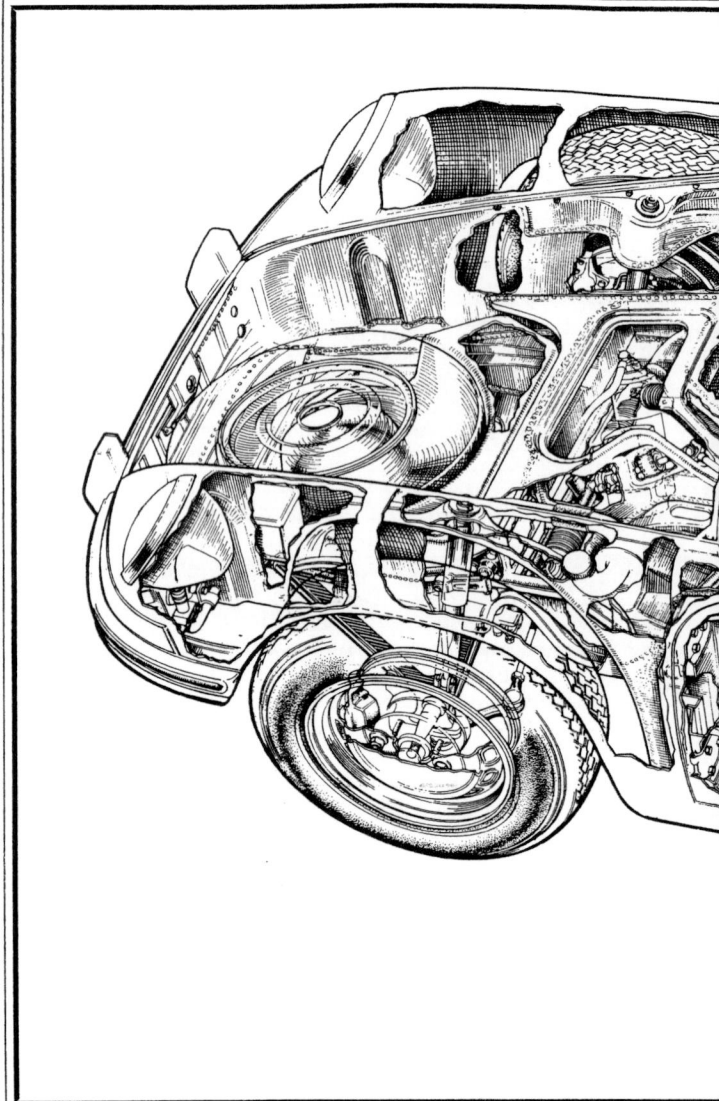

The dashboard is a magnificent edifice. The instrumentation is complete even to an oil *level* gauge (no messy mucking about with a dipstick for the 911 owner). Directly in front of the driver is a huge, 270° electrical tachometer. To its left are gauges for oil and fuel levels, oil pressure and temperatures, and sundry warning lights. On the right are speedometer, odometer, a clock and a few more colorfully flashing lights. About the only thing we didn't like about the dash was the strip of teak running full-width below the instruments. The Porsche people are extremely proud of it, it's supposed to look elegant. It looks as if someone said, "Let's put a strip of teak here; it'll look elegant." It doesn't. If we owned a 911 (dare we dream . . .?), we'd paint it flat black to match the rest of the leatherette-covered dash.

The normal heater, which draws heat from the engine, is supplemented by a gasoline-powered device hidden away under the floor of the trunk compartment. The normal heater, controlled by a small lever just forward of the gearshift, has outlets ahead of each door (which can be closed—or adjusted—by sliding covers), at the base of the windshield and at the rear window. The auxiliary heater, primarily a defroster, draws air from a grille behind the front seats and provides instant heat. It exudes a faint odor of gasoline, but is only used in slow traffic or until the engine warms up. A variable-speed fan circulates air from either heater.

Draft-free ventilation with the windows rolled up is possible at any time of year; fresh air is picked up from the high-pressure area ahead of the windshield, controlled by a lever on the dash, and exhausted through the headliner material and out nearly-invisible slots just above the rear window.

The handbrake is between the front seats, whence it migrated from under the 356's dash. The doors and

Road Research Report: Porsche 911

Importer/manufacturer: Porsche of America Corp.
107 Wren Ave.
Teaneck, N. J.

PRICES
Price as tested: $6490 POE East Coast

ENGINE
Air-cooled, horizontally-opposed 6-cyl, light alloy block, 8 main bearings
Bore x stroke...3.15 x 2.60 in, 80 x 66 mm
Displacement...121.5 cu in, 1991 cc
Compression ratio..9 to one
Carburetion...6 Solex 40 PI
Valve gear....................1 overhead camshaft per bank of cylinders
Valve diameter..............................Intake 1.54 in, exhaust 1.38 in
Valve lift..Intake 0.451 in, exhaust 0.412 in
Valve timing (at 1 mm checking clearance; operating clearance is .1 mm)
  Intake opens..29 BTC
  Intake closes..39 ABC
  Exhaust opens..39 BBC
  Exhaust closes...19 ATC
Power (SAE)...148 bhp @ 6100 rpm
Torque...140 lbs-ft @ 4200 rpm
Specific power output.....................1.22 hp per cu in, 74 hp per liter
Usable range of engine speeds.....................1000–6800 rpm
Electrical system................12-Volt, 45 amp-hr battery, A.C. generator
Fuel recommended...Premium
Mileage..16–24 mpg
Range on 15.5-gallon tank...............................248–372 miles

DRIVE TRAIN
Clutch...8.5-inch single dry plate
Transmission..5-speed

Gear	Ratio	Over-all	mph/1000 rpm	Max mph
Rev	2.69	11.911	−6.0	−41
1st	2.833	12.535	6.5	44
2nd	1.778	7.873	9.5	65
3rd	1.218	5.393	13.7	93
4th	0.962	4.259	17.3	118
5th	0.821	3.635	20.3	138 (theoretical)

Final drive ratio...4.428 to one

CHASSIS
Wheelbase...87.1 in
Track...F 52.7, R 51.9 in
Length..164 in
Width..63.4 in
Height...51.9 in
Ground clearance..5.9 in
Dry weight...2177 lbs
Curb weight...2376 lbs
Test weight..2566 lbs
Weight distribution front/rear...........................40/60%
Pounds per bhp (test weight)...........................17.36
Suspension F: Ind., MacPherson strut and lower wishbone, telescopic
  dampers, longitudinal torsion bars, anti-roll bar
  R: Ind., semi-trailing arms, transverse torsion bars, telescopic dampers
Brakes.........Ate-Dunlop discs, 10.8-in discs front, 11.3-in discs rear,
376 sq in swept area
Steering..ZF rack and pinion
Turns, lock to lock..2.8
Turning circle...33 ft 9 in
Tires...165 x 15 Dunlop SP
Revs per mile...808

MAINTENANCE
Crankcase capacity...8 qts (dry sump)
Oil change interval..3000 miles
Grease fittings..0

ACCELERATION
Zero to	Seconds
30 mph	2.3
40 mph	3.3
50 mph	5.2
60 mph	7.0
70 mph	9.8
80 mph	12.4
90 mph	15.6
100 mph	20.0
Standing ¼-mile	90 mph in 15.6

Above, the 901 engine of the prototype; below, the 911 production engine. The primary difference is in the carburetion; the 901 used two triple-throat Solex carburetors, the 911 uses six single-throat Solexes. The factory has quoted 130 DIN horsepower for both engines, but we suspect that this may be on the low side; it's probably more like the 148 SAE hp figure. The single overhead cam and rocker arms are easily seen in the above drawing, though only part of the chain drive is shown. The ram tubes (or "velocity stacks") are fitted to the production engines, hidden under the air-cleaner.

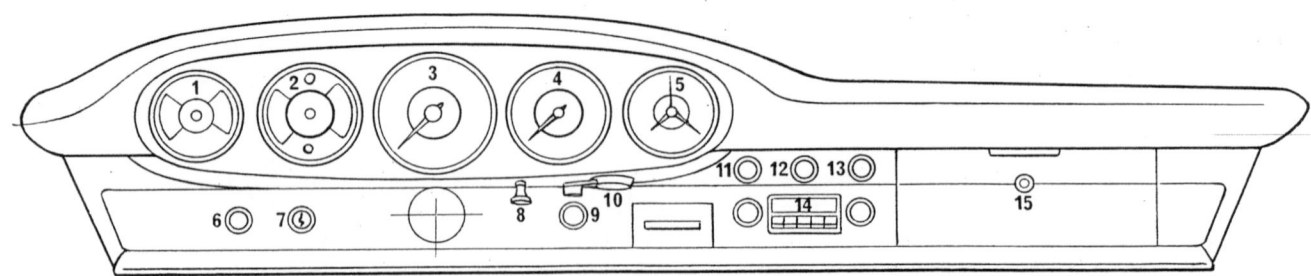

(1) Fuel level and oil level, (2) oil temperature and pressure, (3) tachometer, (4) speedometer, odometer and tripmeter, (5) clock, (6) lights, (7) ignition, (8) tripmeter return, (9) cigarette lighter, (10) fresh air control, (11) fog lights switch, (12) parking lights, (13) auxiliary heater and fan control, (14) optional radio, (15) glove compartment. Warning lights in (2), (3) and (4) indicate: turn signals on, oil pressure low, hand brake on, and malfunction in the electrical system.

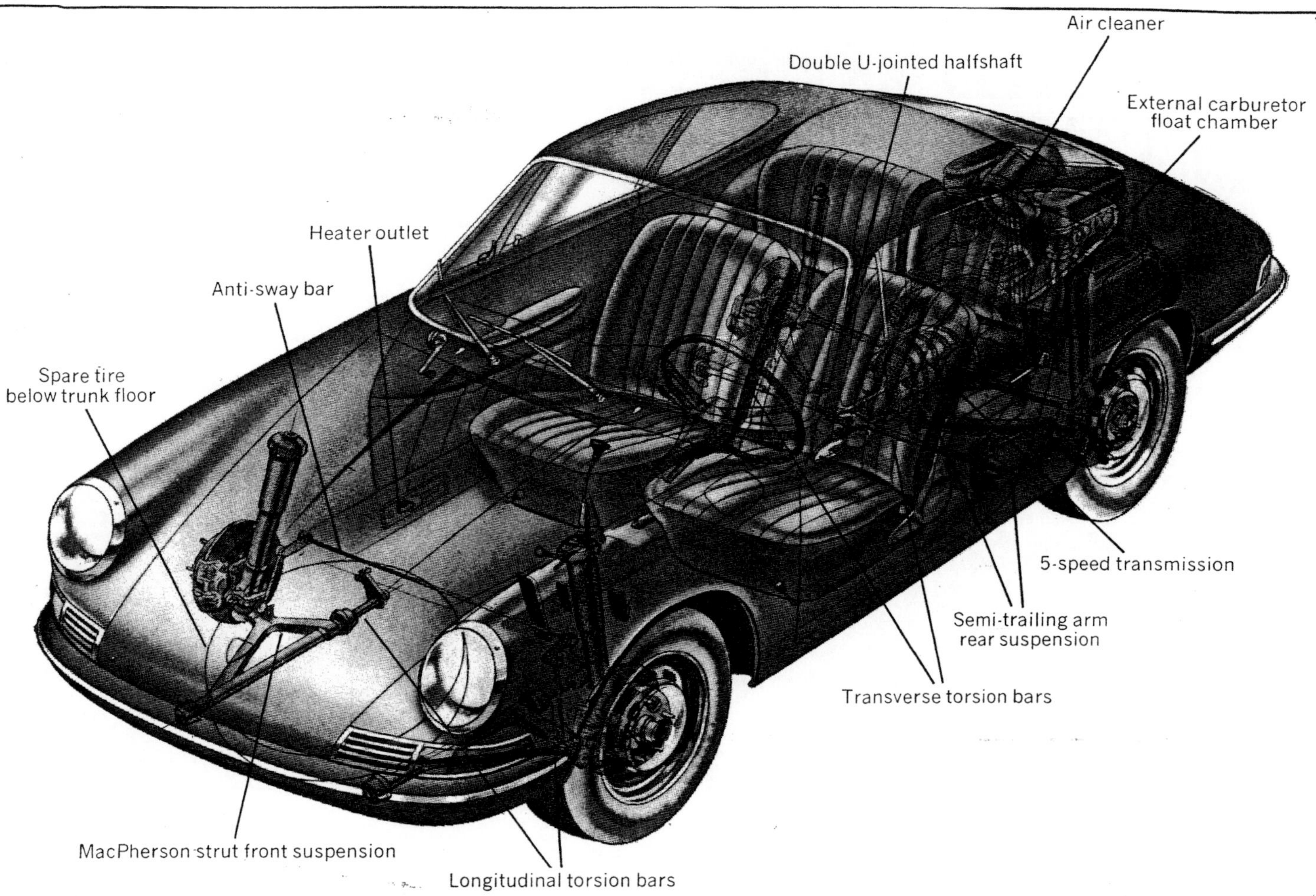

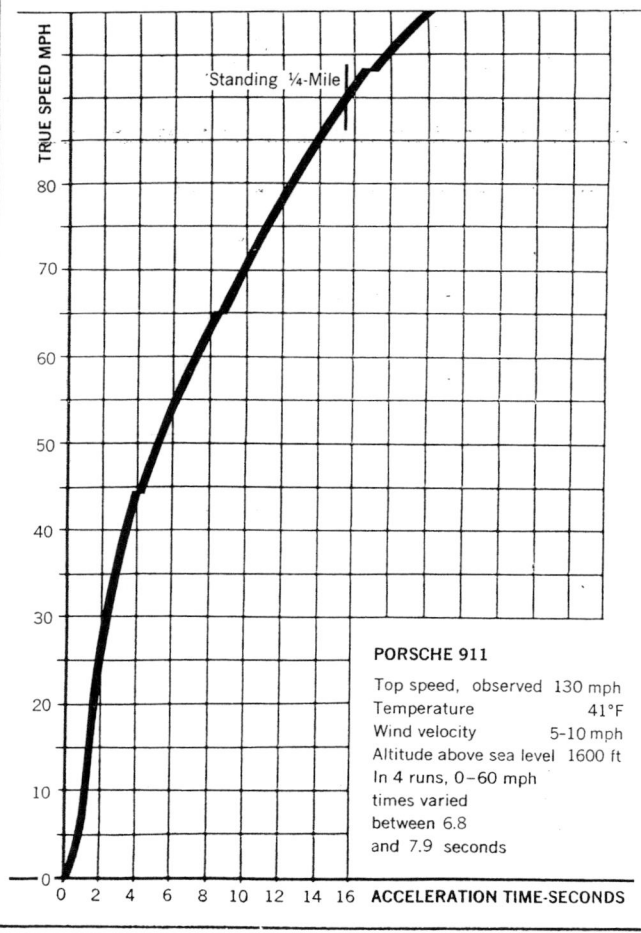

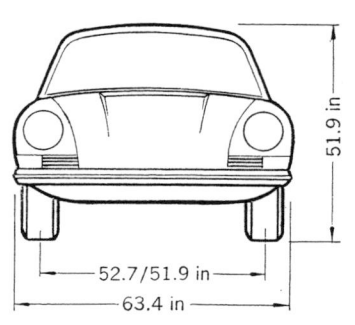

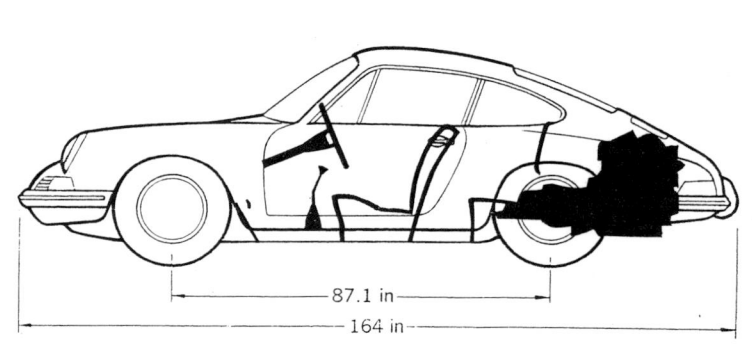

Air cleaner
Double U-jointed halfshaft
External carburetor float chamber
Heater outlet
Anti-sway bar
Spare tire below trunk floor
5-speed transmission
Semi-trailing arm rear suspension
Transverse torsion bars
MacPherson strut front suspension
Longitudinal torsion bars

TRUE SPEED MPH
Standing ¼-Mile
80
70
60
50
40
30
20
10
0
0 2 4 6 8 10 12 14 16 ACCELERATION TIME-SECONDS
PORSCHE 911
Top speed, observed 130 mph
Temperature 41°F
Wind velocity 5-10 mph
Altitude above sea level 1600 ft
In 4 runs, 0–60 mph times varied between 6.8 and 7.9 seconds

51.9 in
52.7/51.9 in
63.4 in

87.1 in
164 in

Autocar ROAD TEST NUMBER 2101

PORSCHE 911S 1,991 c.c.

AT A GLANCE: Outstanding 2-litre GT with sparkling acceleration and high top speed. Exceptionally light controls with fade-free brakes and excellent steering. Normally good road-holding in the dry, but needs care in the wet. Comfortable ride and seating with restricted room in the back for occasional passengers. Well finished, high precision car.

MANUFACTURER
Porschestrasse, Stuttgart-Zuffenhausen, Germany.

BRITISH CONCESSIONAIRES
Porsche Cars (Great Britain), Ltd., Falcon Works, London Road, Isleworth, Middlesex.

PRICES
Basic	£2,892 0s 0d
Purchase Tax	£664 9s 5d
Total (in G.B.)	£3,556 9s 5d

EXTRAS
Lap and diagonal seat belts, per pair .. £9 10s 0d

PERFORMANCE SUMMARY
Mean maximum speed	137 m.p.h.
Standing start ¼-mile	15·8 sec
0-60 m.p.h.	8·0 sec
30-70 m.p.h.	7·3 sec
Overall fuel consumption	15·7 m.p.g.
Miles per tankful	215

RELATING production cars to their competition prototypes is usually a doubtful process, and often there is little direct evidence of the lessons learnt on the track. With GT cars, however, there is frequently an indefinable feel which may or may not be bred into the machine by the influence of successful performance at the limit. In the case of Porsche the position is different from most, because the original 911 contained many features from their remarkable racing cars, such as controlled suspension geometry, disc brakes and a flat-6 overhead-cam dry-sump engine.

As production of this high-performance machine gained momentum, a tamer version called the 912 was introduced, with the familiar flat-4 engine; we published a full road test on 24 September 1965. Earlier this year we travelled to the Hockenheim circuit in Germany to be driven in a new GT racing car, the Carrera 6, which was powered by a very "hot" version of the same flat-6 911 engine. A few months later the 911S production car was announced with a net power of 160 b.h.p., 30 more than the ordinary (if such a car can ever be called ordinary) 911 and 55 less than the racer. And from the moment the engine fires one is left in no doubt of its impressive pedigree.

Like all other Porsches, the 911S has no choke for cold starting, but the usual technique of pumping the accelerator for a rich mixture must be avoided on this one, as the six chokes of the Weber carburettors then wet the induction too much. All that is needed is a turn of the ignition key and perhaps half throttle, whereupon the engine bursts to life instantly, hot or cold. Outside is the characteristic waffle and hammer of air-cooled cylinders, but inside the car the predominant noise is an exciting, high-pitched whine of camshaft gears.

Free-revving Engine

Blipping the throttle at rest sends the rev counter needle catapulting round the dial just like on a racing car, indicating a light flywheel and tremendous torque. On the road in the lower gears practically the same thing happens and one must keep a very wary eye indeed on the red blob at 7,300 r.p.m. Over-revving can damage the valve gear, so Porsche very wisely fit an ignition cut-out on the rotor arm to operate at exactly 7,300 r.p.m. We know it is accurate because we checked the rev counter against our fifth-wheel speedometer. Once or twice we reached the limit on the road without realizing it when concentrating on rapid overtaking.

Autocar Road Test 2101

MAKE: **PORSCHE**

TYPE: **911S**

Speed range, gear ratios and time in seconds

m.p.h.	Top (3·5)	Fourth (4·6)	Third (5·8)	Second (8·3)	First (13·6)
10—30	—	—	—	4·4	2·5
20—40	—	8·2	5·8	4·6	2·4
30—50	11·6	7·8	5·4	3·5	—
40—60	12·0	7·5	5·2	3·4	—
50—70	11·9	6·8	5·0	—	—
60—80	11·5	6·7	5·0	—	—
70—90	11·9	6·9	5·7	—	—
80—100	12·7	6·7	—	—	—
90—110	14·2	7·1	—	—	—
100—120	17·6	—	—	—	—

WEIGHT
Kerb weight (with oil and half-full fuel tank): 20·9 cwt (2,345lb-1,047kg)
Front-rear distribution, per cent F, 41·5; R, 58·5
Laden as tested 23·9 cwt (2,681lb-1,215kg)

TURNING CIRCLES
Between kerbs .. L, 34ft 2in.; R, 32ft 2in.
Between walls .. L, 35ft 10in.; R, 33ft 10in.
Steering wheel turns, lock to lock .. .. 2·7

PERFORMANCE DATA
Top gear m.p.h. per 1,000 r.p.m. .. 20·4
Mean piston speed at max. power 2,860ft/min
Engine revs at mean max. speed .. 6,650 r.p.m.
B.h.p. per ton laden 134

OIL CONSUMPTION
SAE 10W/30 .. .. 860 miles per pint

FUEL CONSUMPTION
At constant speeds
30 m.p.h. 40·5 m.p.g.   70 m.p.h. 29·3 m.p.g.
40 ,, 37·1 ,,   80 ,,   26·4 ,,
50 ,, 32·8 ,,   90 ,,   23·5 ,,
60 ,, 31·7 ,,   100 ,,   19·6 ,,
Overall m.p.g. .... 15·7 (18·0 litres/100km)
Normal range m.p.g. 15-25 (18·8-11·3 litres/100km)
Test distance .. .. .. 1,530 miles
Estimated (DIN) m.p.g. 26·7 (10·6 litres/100km)
Grade .. .. Premium (96·8-98·8 RM)

TEST CONDITIONS
Weather .. Sunny with showers, with 10-20 m.p.h. wind
Temperature .. .. 58 deg.C (14 deg.F.)
Barometer .. .. 29·3 in.Hg.
Surfaces .. Dry with wet patches, concrete and asphalt

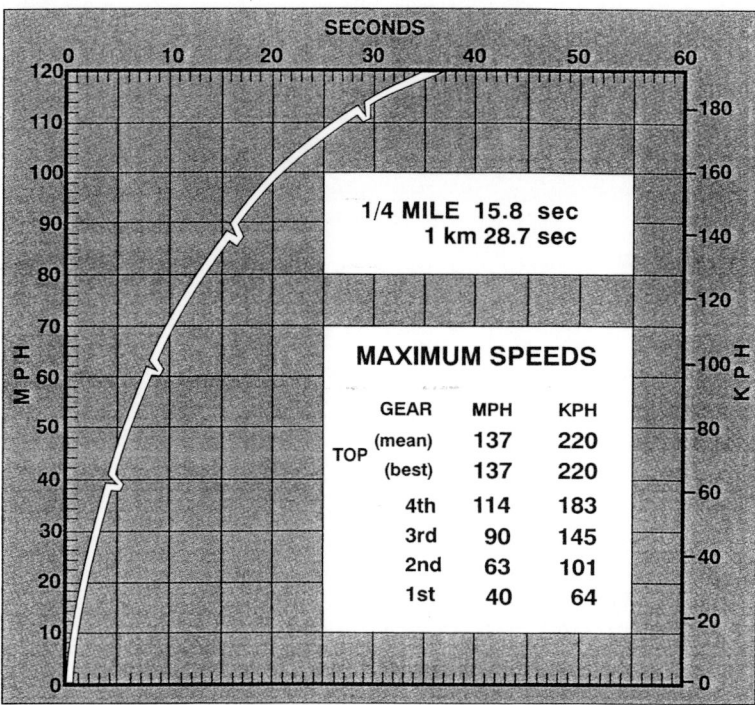

1/4 MILE 15.8 sec
1 km 28.7 sec

MAXIMUM SPEEDS

GEAR		MPH	KPH
TOP	(mean)	137	220
	(best)	137	220
4th		114	183
3rd		90	145
2nd		63	101
1st		40	64

TIME IN SECONDS	3·0	4·2	6·1	8·0	10·3	12·7	15·9	20·5	25·5	37·7
TRUE SPEED MPH	30	40	50	60	70	80	90	100	110	120
INDICATED MPH	33	44	55	66	76	87	97	107	117	127

BRAKES Pedal load Retardation Equiv. distance
(from 30 m.p.h. in neutral)
25lb   0·30g   100ft
50lb   0·55g   55ft
75lb   0·75g   40ft
100lb 0·95g   31·7ft
Handbrake 0·20g   150ft

CLUTCH Pedal load and travel 28lb and 5·5in.

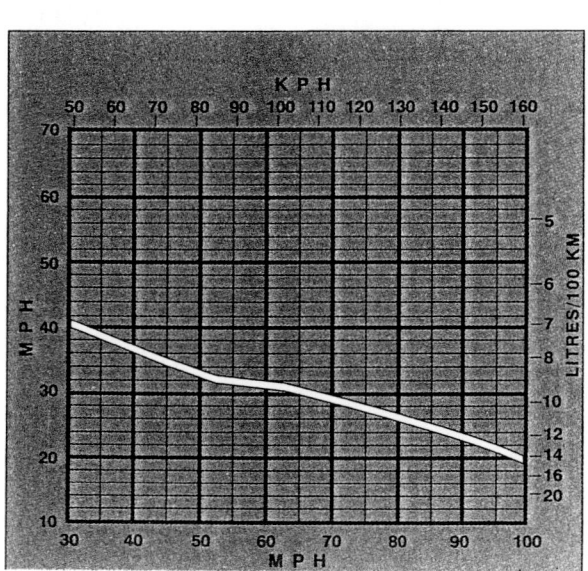

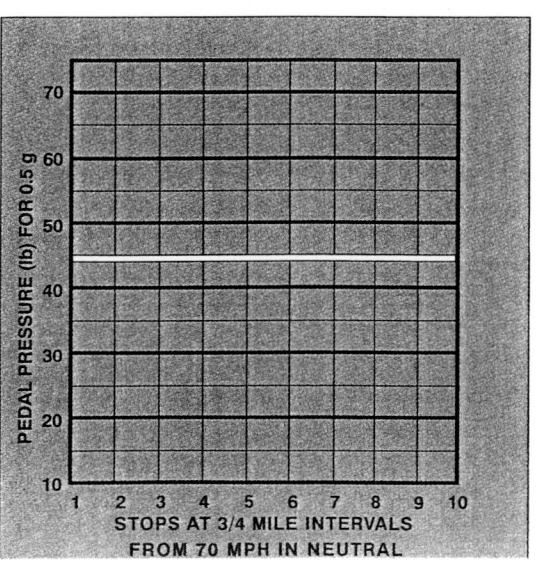

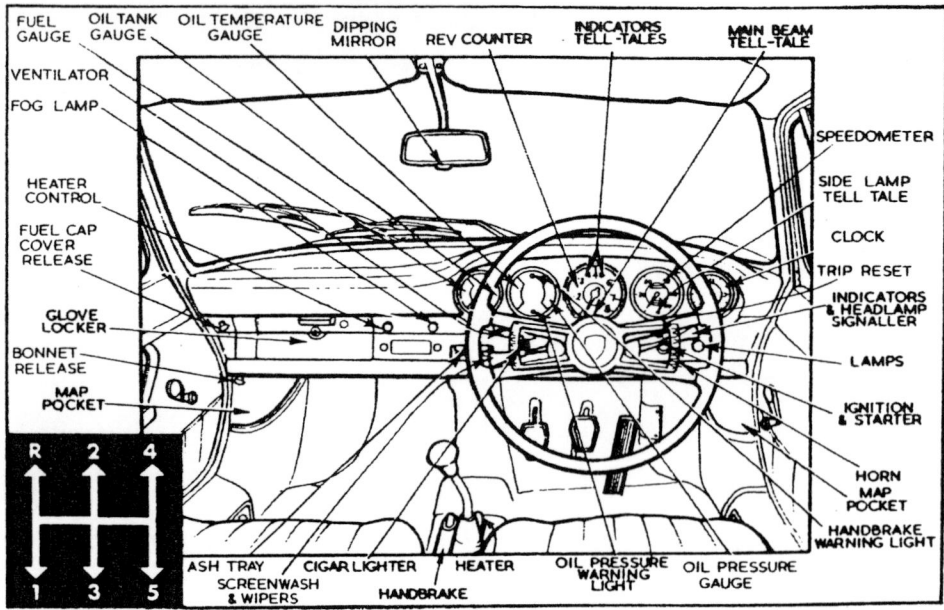

When accelerating through the gears, two definite steps in the torque curve can be felt. The catalogue peak comes at 5,200 r.p.m., but before that at about 3,000 the engine takes a deep breath and literally surges up to the next step, where the extra punch feels like an additional pair of cylinders being switched in. This kick in the back leaves passengers unaccustomed to it slightly winded, and it is sudden enough to cause momentary wheelspin on wet surfaces, even in third.

Once familiar with the car, one keeps the rev counter needle within this punchy band of 3,000 to 7,000 r.p.m. with the aid of the superb 5-speed gearbox when driving fast. On the move, only the upper four ratios are needed and these are arranged in a conventional H-pattern gate without spring loading. First and reverse are away to the left, with quite a strong spring-resisted movement that way, and a firm action is needed to snatch bottom when very slow traffic gets in the way.

Gears and speeds

Ratios are spaced evenly over the lower four, but fifth is much higher for cruising. At a leisurely 4,500 r.p.m. the car is running happily at just under 100 m.p.h., which seemed to be a comfortable gait for long stretches of *autobahnen*. Above 120 m.p.h. acceleration tails off and it took several miles to reach the maximum of 137 m.p.h. This speed was repeated, incidentally, four times in opposite directions and held for mile after mile without quavering nor any signs of the engine tiring or overheating. Porsche claim that with more breaking-in (the test car had covered only 2,900 miles when these measurements were made) a top speed of over 140 m.p.h. can be expected. We can think of no reason for doubting this.

At maximum speed the Porsche held a very true course, despite a lot of uneven bumps in the road surface; on another day, with strong side gusts, there were only slight deflections to a degree that was noticeable but not a worry.

Standing start acceleration times showed a remarkable consistency, despite a stiff force 4 breeze. Runs in the same direction could be repeated to within 0·4sec right up to about 115 m.p.h., which was reached in under a mile from rest. Some damp patches on the road helped the getaway, as we were able to keep the engine right on the peak of its torque curve while the wheels spun for some five yards or so leaving black streaks through the moisture. The urgent crescendo rising in pitch from the engine was very like a jet aircraft making a take-off run and the inertia forces felt every bit as strong.

Steering

The steering of the Porsche is outstandingly light and very high geared. Even when parking, the neat leather-covered wheel can be spun from lock to lock with very little effort, whereas on main roads and country lanes it becomes quite delightful. There is a slight rubbery ▶

A massive air cleaner feeds the two triple-choke carburettors. On the right is the oil filler cap for the dry-sump lubrication system

Gold lettering and a neat "911S" under the air intake grille show which model this is

feel to movements, not the vague kind but the well-insulated type that absorbs the feed-back from bumps and ruts and takes none of the precision away. The front of the car responds instantly to commands, as we were comforted to confirm when a jay-walking pedestrian stepped in our path at point-blank range.

On two other occasions we had cause to be grateful we were in the Porsche. In traffic, the car behind nudged our rubber-faced over-riders without leaving a mark, and (unusual for a non-servo all-disc system) the brakes bit instantly from only 10 m.p.h. when another car changed lanes unexpectedly.

Brakes

The brakes are indeed exceptionally light, much more so than on the 912 tested before, because the ventilated wheels allow softer pads to run cooler. Less than 100lb on the pedal is enough to lock the wheels on a dry road and produce 0·95g retardation. There was no trace of fade at all during 10 stops from 70 m.p.h. and during a lot of faster driving abroad we always had confidence that the Porsche would stop as quickly as possible, as often as we wished. If anything, the brakes become slightly more sensitive as they heat up and they can be really hammered in rally style driving without any signs of distress.

Small drums are built into the rear disc hubs for the handbrake, which is designed for parking more than emergency stopping. Only a light pull on the central lever is enough to hold the car firmly facing up a 1-in-3 hill (facing down on a damp surface, the car dragged its locked wheels forwards), but from 30 m.p.h. we recorded only a poor 0·2g. Normally the handbrake is never used on the move, so it could be that the linings had never bedded in.

In keeping with the rest of the controls, the clutch is exceptionally light and requires only 28lb to disengage it. It has a smooth progressive take-up and never showed any signs of slipping, even during full power gearchanges.

The handling of the 911S is rather different from that of the 912. In the 912 one could abuse the car almost limitlessly and never get into trouble. With something not far short of double the horsepower, the 911S is not a car for the novice and even the experienced fast driver must slow down when the road turns wet. Initially there is stable understeer on corners, but power oversteer can be brought in with the right foot to any required degree. The driver needs to know the car well and what he is about.

Roadholding

On the road, the 911S feels evenly balanced and well set-up, and it takes corners practically flat without any noticeable roll. In the dry the adhesion is little short of phenomenal and one can hurtle through twisty lanes almost without touching the brakes simply by snatching the right one of the five gears for each turn that appears.

In the wet the power available is

The five-spoked light alloy wheels are a distinguishing feature of the 911S. The foglamps are in special recesses under the bumper panel

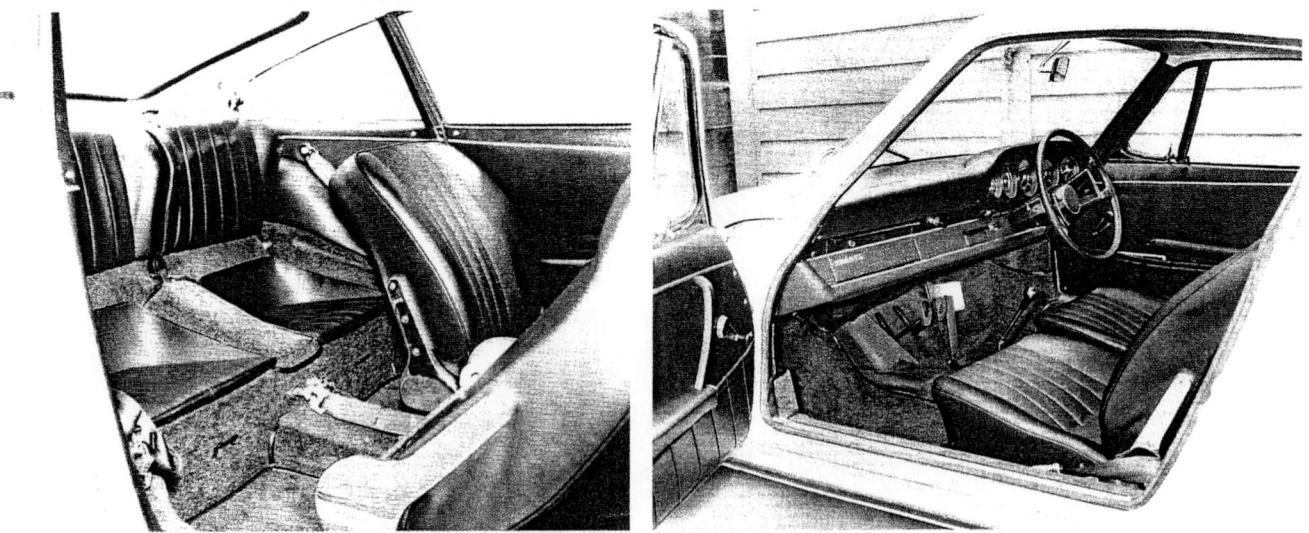

Left: The rear seats are small and headroom is limited; the individual backrests fold flat to give more luggage space. Right: A very neat instrument panel is used, with the dials angled towards the driver's eyes. The steering wheel is leather-covered

HOW THE PORSCHE 911S COMPARES:

TOTAL PRICE		MAXIMUM SPEED (mean) M.P.H.	0-60 M.P.H. SECONDS	M.P.G. Overall	STANDING START ¼ MILE (secs)
£3,556	Porsche 911S				
£3,051	Alfa Romeo 2600 sprint				
£3,588	Mercedes-Benz 230SL				
£1,126	Austin-Healey 3000 Mk III				
£2,284	Jaguar E-type 2+2				

too much even for the excellent German Dunlop SP tyres, and the wheels spin all too easily in first and second gears. One needs to feed the throttles open carefully and progressively to prevent the tail twitching about and to treat the polished surfaces in towns with considerable discretion.

Ride Comfort

The ride and comfort of the 911S are excellent, with a clever co-ordination of seat springing and suspension rates. The well-shaped seats hold their occupants against the very high cornering forces and most of the time they give a "dead" response to vertical disturbances. Only at slow town speeds does the ride become slightly joggy, and on the open road the Porsche storms along over rough and smooth alike with hardly a tremor. On the *pavé* we were able to bounce about at 40 m.p.h. without any rattles or vibrations in the body structure, and there was a particularly impressive lack of suspension crashing.

Even though the 911S engine is only a 2-litre unit, and it is difficult to remember this when judging the performance, its considerable power is given at the expense of fuel consumption and our overall figure was 15·7 m.p.g. At steady speeds the high gearing and good aerodynamic shape give much more reasonable figures, with nearly 30 m.p.g. at 70 m.p.h. Human nature being what it is, however, there would be no point in having the car if one did not drive it to the best advantage, and few owners indeed will do better than the 17·8 m.p.g. we returned under normal conditions after we had settled into the second week of our all too short "ownership."

The driving position is well up to the nature of the car, with rake adjustment for the seat back and all controls within fingertip reach of the wheel. A broad span of circular instruments spreads in an arc in front of the driver's eyes and the steering wheel has a narrow X-spoke pattern to prevent obstructions. In the centre of the dials is the largest and most important, the rev counter reading to 8,000 r.p.m. On the right of this is a slightly smaller 150 m.p.h. speedometer with rather sparse markings at 30 m.p.h. intervals. This instrument had a large degree of optimism—7 m.p.h. from 70 m.p.h. through to 130 m.p.h.—unnecessary in a car which is *genuinely* so fast.

Instruments

To the right of the speedometer is an accurate clock with a red pointer which can be set, say, at the estimated time of arrival on a journey. On the left of the rev counter is a pair of double-function dials, the first one giving oil conditions—temperature and pressure—and the second, smaller one the contents of the petrol and oil tanks. The indicator switch on the right of the steering column flashes main beams when pulled (unless sidelamps are lit, then it flashes dipped beams) and undips the lamps when pushed. The main lighting master switch is on the right of the facia.

Matching the indicator lever, on ▶

the left of the column, is the control for the three-speed wipers (we timed 30, 40 and 50 strokes per min. in a thunderstorm), which when pulled operates the four-jet electric screen washers.

Although the rear compartment is intended largely as a luggage platform, we did open the midget rear seats on several occasions and carry back seat passengers, once for a 40-mile Sunday afternoon outing There were no serious complaints of being unduly cramped, but clambering in and out is an ungraceful business for both sexes.

Summing up a car like the 911S is not easy, because one must single out individual features from an integrated design. Without a doubt, the engine is the most impressive part, with its almost unbelievable smoothness and urgent willingness for continuous hard work. One should also mention the superb lightness of all the controls which, together with excellent seating, immediately put the driver at-one with the car and enable him to go out and enjoy its character to the full. The Porsche 911S is a car one never likes to leave parked when one could be driving it somewhere.

SPECIFICATION: PORSCHE 911S, REAR ENGINE, REAR-WHEEL DRIVE

ENGINE
- Cylinders .. 6, horizontally opposed
- Cooling system .. Ducted air and fan
- Bore .. 80mm (3·15in.)
- Stroke .. 66mm (2·60in.)
- Displacement .. 1,991 c.c. (121·5 cu in.)
- Valve gear .. Single overhead camshaft, one per bank
- Compression ratio 9·8-to-1
- Carburettors .. 2 Weber 40 IDA 3C.
- Fuel pump .. Bendix electric
- Oil filter .. Purolator 3C 34 full flow
- Max. power .. 160 b.h.p. (net) at 6,600 r.p.m.
- Max. torque .. 132 lb ft (net) at 5,200 r.p.m.

TRANSMISSION
- Clutch .. Fichtel and Sachs single dry plate diaphragm spring 8·5in. dia.
- Gearbox .. Five speeds, all synchromesh
- Gear ratios .. Top 0·79; Fourth 1·04; Third 1·32; Second 1·89; First 3·09; Reverse 2·69
- Final drive .. Spiral bevel, 4·43 to 1

SUSPENSION
- Front .. Independent, MacPherson struts and lower wishbones; longitudinal torsion bars and adjustable telescopic dampers; anti-roll bar
- Rear .. Independent, semi-trailing arms and transverse torsion bars; telescopic dampers; anti-roll bar

CHASSIS AND BODY
- Construction .. Integral with steel body

STEERING
- Type .. ZF rack and pinion
- Turns, lock-to-lock 2·7. Wheel dia. 16·5in.

BRAKES
- Make and type .. Dunlop ATE4 discs, handbrake drums incorporated in rear discs
- Dimensions .. F, 10·6in.dia., discs. R, 11·0in.dia., discs
- Swept area .. F, 183 sq in., R, 177 sq in. Total 360 sq in. (307 sq in. per ton laden)

WHEELS
- Type .. Forged light alloy 4·5in. wide rim
- Tyres .. Dunlop SP CB57 tubed
- Size .. 165 HR—15in.

EQUIPMENT
- Battery .. 12-volt, 45-amp hr
- Alternator .. Bosch K1/14V/35A/20
- Headlamps .. Bosch asymmetric 45/40 watt
- Reversing lamp .. 2 standard
- Electric fuses .. 12
- Screen wipers .. 3-speed, self-parking
- Screen washer .. Standard electric
- Interior heater .. Standard, ducted hot air
- Safety belts .. Extra, anchorages provided
- Interior trim .. PVC seats, PVC headlining
- Floor covering .. Nylon carpet with rubber reinforcement
- Starting handle .. No provision
- Jack .. Friction pillar
- Jacking points .. 2 each side under sills
- Other bodies .. Targa convertible

MAINTENANCE
- Fuel tank .. 13·7 Imp. gallons (low level warning light) (62 litres)
- Engine sump .. 16 pints (9 litres), SAE HD30 Summer; HD20 Winter Change oil every 6,000 miles; change filter element every 6,000 miles
- Gearbox and final drive .. 5·5 pints SAE 90, change oil every 6,000 miles
- Grease .. None required
- Tyre pressures .. F, 26; R, 29 p.s.i. (normal driving) F, 31; R, 34 p.s.i. (fast driving) F, 31; R, 34 p.s.i. (full load)

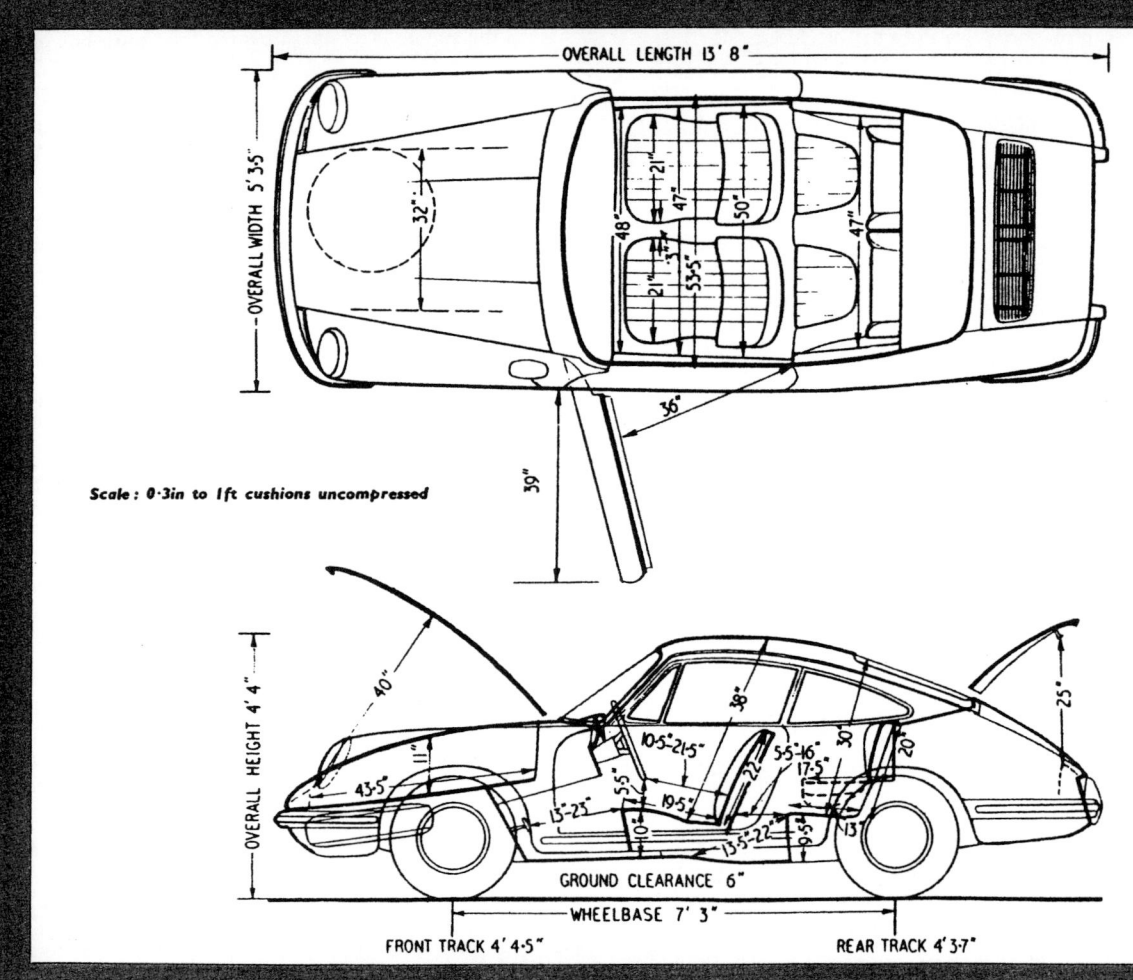

Scale: 0·3in to 1ft cushions uncompressed

On the Road with a Porsche Type 911

JUST before the Government clamped the 70 m.p.h. limit on this unhappy motoring country of ours, the Porsche Concessionaires for Great Britain said they could let us have a 911 on loan. As luck would have it the Editor was rather busily engaged with other road-test cars so he suggested that I might like the Porsche. There were two other reasons as well, which were that (a) I had driven well over a quarter of a million miles in Porsches over the past 10 years, so I should know something about Porsches, and (b) the 911 was the model I had marked down as my 1965 car until economic and policy reasons caused me to change my ideas and have a 4.2-litre E-type Jaguar instead.

After covering some 1,200 miles in a week, most of them at fairly high speeds, a report on the 911 Porsche is the easiest thing to write, for without question it is the best car Porsche have yet built for normal road use. However, if I finish the road test here and now by merely saying " this is one of the best cars I have ever driven," and leave it at that, the Production Manager will start ticking and complain about empty pages, while the more inquisitive readers will be asking " Why is it one of the best cars you have ever driven ?", so I will now try and analyse one of the best week's motoring that I have had for a long time.

The Porsche 911 is the 2-litre flat-six-cylinder engine car which first appeared over a year ago, and was a complete break-away from the old 356 series that was derived from Volkswagens way back in 1950/51. Apart from being an entirely different shape from the accepted beetle-like Porsches of old, the 911 was the first production break from swing axle suspension at the rear and trailing-arm links at the front, although torsion bars are still retained. The front suspension uses a Macpherson-strut layout and wishbone, and wide-base triangular trailing members support each rear wheel completely independently. The engine is air-cooled, like all Porsches, and is a horizontally opposed six-cylinder, with three cylinders to each bank, the inclined overhead valves being operated by rockers from an overhead camshaft

Good looks. The 911 Porsche has attractive lines and is a true GT car. Here it is parked in a quiet village square in Castle Hedingham.

layout, the camshaft on each bank being driven by chain from the crankshaft, while a belt drives a multi-blade fan that blows air through ducts downwards onto the cylinder barrels and heads, the air then being ducted out underneath the car. As on previous Porsches the engine is mounted behind the centre-line of the rear axle, though, unlike the 4-cylinder Porsches, this power unit is supported at both ends, the front on the gearbox/axle unit and the rear on a transverse mounting. The gearbox is a 5-speed and reverse unit, which lies ahead of the rear axle centre-line. Disc brakes are fitted to all four wheels, and the test car was shod with German Dunlop SP tyres. When this model was first released by the factory it was known as the 901, and was due to be followed by the sports/racing 904, but due to various reasons the 904 appeared first, and when the 901 eventually got into production it was renumbered the 911. This can be pronounced " nine-eleven " or " nine-one-one " the former being the more usual name for the car. The same car, fitted with a push-rod 4-cylinder engine is also available and is known as the 912, but our interest lies in the high-performance 911 model.

On first acquaintance the car seemed a little disappointing, having no particular character about the interior when you first sit down, unlike the old 356 series, which you felt could only be Porsches. Driving quietly away this lack of character was even more noticeable, so that seasoned Porsche owners commented that it was all right, but hardly a Porsche, and in fact it could have been almost any sort of reasonable GT car. But once I had sorted out all the controls, found my way about the car and got out into the open country the whole car immediately became alive and was unmistakably a Porsche in all the true traditions of the Stuttgart firm. The more I drove it and the harder I made it work the more Porsche-like it became, so that by the end of the week I had no doubts at all that this was a car from the brains of Dr. Porsche and his men, and could not possibly have come from anywhere else, and I was continually saying to myself " Why don't all manufacturers make cars like this ? It can't be so difficult."

The most outstanding attribute of a Porsche is the remarkable one-piece feel of the whole structure, for no matter what sort of surface you are on, or what speed you are travelling at, you never get the feeling that anything other than the suspension is moving. There is no kick-back through the steering wheel, no movement of the doors, seats or body structure, and you never get the feeling that something is going to fall off. In short, the whole car has a feeling that it is indestructible, unlike many other cars in the GT category in which you feel that even if the exhaust system doesn't rattle off, the doors will fly open, or the bodywork begin to split somewhere. This one-piece feel in the 911 is coupled with suspension, ride, road-holding, steering, braking and general good manners that are truly modern, and the nearest to perfection that production cars have yet reached. The steering looks, on paper, to be unnecessarily complicated, and unlikely to provide good

Engine room. The engine compartment of the 911 is packed. Visible here is the belt driven cooling fan, the air intake and air cleaners and the throttle linkage. Note the neat rear lighting that merges into the body shape.

results, but it has set a new standard in my estimation, even better than the 230SL Mercedes-Benz power steering, which used to be my idea of the best. The Porsche has a very short steering column, from which a universal joint takes the motion to the centre of the car and then another universal joint couples to a shaft incorporating a flexible damper joint, which operates the rack and pinion mechanism which itself is mounted rigidly on a tubular cross-member. The short primary column from the steering wheel is carried in a tubular housing that tapers into a flat plate at its forward end, where it is bolted to the body/chassis structure. In the event of a head-on crash into a solid object this housing will collapse and the driver does not get four feet of steel tube through his chest, as with a normal steering column assembly. There is absolutely no lost motion in the system and you can feel exactly what the wheels are doing at all times, without any of the usual "kick-back" associated with rack and pinion steering. The actual steering characteristics are almost complete neutrality, and I never achieved cornering powers on the open road that would cause the 911 to show signs of breakaway at either the front or the rear, and, believe me, the German SP tyres, which the Porsche suspension kept firmly on the road, can absorb some pretty high cornering forces. On a closed aerodrome it was possible to reach the limit, and then the rear went first, as with most cars, but under normal fast road-driving there is little indication that the engine weight is overhung at the rear. Since the first of the 911s was built, one of which I tried in 1964 round the Solitude circuit, the amount of roll has been reduced enormously. The early cars seemed to roll on an axis parallel with the ground, rather like a DS Citroën, but this trait has now disappeared.

Truly outstanding about the Porsche 911 are the "ride" characteristics, which smooth out road surfaces in a most impressive manner and put the car in the same category as Citroën and Rover 2000. It is the sort of level ride that all family saloons of good quality should have, but very few achieve, and Porsche have it in a pure GT car. Along a local "test" road which has a bumpy and wavy surface, where 60-65 m.p.h. is good going in most cars, the Porsche was quite happy at 85-90 m.p.h. One of the secrets of good suspension is shock-absorbers, and the telescopic shockers on the Porsche have progressively-acting rubber buffers inside them.

Every year the list of manufacturers who use Porsche baulk-ring syncromesh patents in their gearbox designs gets bigger and bigger, and it makes you realise that Porsche must know something about gearboxes. Anyone who has driven the old Type 356 cars will appreciate the Porsche gearbox, and the 5-speed box that followed the various versions of 4-speed on the earlier cars takes over where the old ones left off. The present 5-speed gearbox is truly fantastic and you find yourself changing gear just for the fun of the thing, or to "show off" to your friends. An accompanying illustration shows the layout of the gear-lever positions, and the lever has to be pressed against a spring to get 1st or reverse, so that when changing from 1st into 2nd you merely apply a forward pressure. If you apply any sideways force you can almost guarantee that you will change from 1st to 4th. I let four friends try the car on a sprint course, and two muffed their first change and two didn't. Porsche have never built cars that require any brute force, finesse in driving being assumed to be a natural talent for Porsche owners. From 2nd to 3rd you can pull the lever back as fast as you like, and then the change from 3rd across the gate to 4th is one of those outstanding things in motoring. If you are on full power in 3rd, with 6,800 r.p.m. on the tachometer, you can flash the lever across into 4th as fast as possible, but you must press the clutch pedal sufficiently to free the plates.

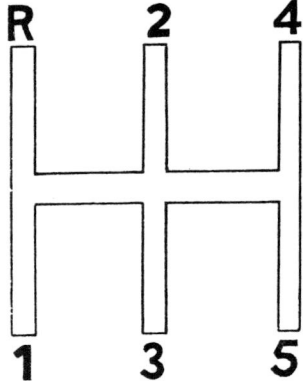

The layout of the five-speed Porsche 911 gearbox.

BONNET SPACE.—The spacious luggage compartment under the bonnet of the 911. The shaped fuel tank has the spare wheel fitted into it.

The hard, crisp exhaust note as you continue on at full throttle in 4th gear is sheer heaven. Vintage enthusiasts get enormous pleasure from a rapid clutchless-change on a crash gearbox, being able to demonstrate their prowess, but the change at peak r.p.m. from 3rd to 4th in a Porsche 911 will match any such pleasures, and what is more you are beginning to travel pretty quickly by this time. The change into fifth is similar to that from 2nd to 3rd. For most road work there is no need to use 1st gear, other than for starting off from rest, for providing the wheels are actually rolling the car will pull away well in 2nd gear; consequently you can treat the gearbox as a 4-speed unit, with an emergency low gear, but it is a close-ratio, high-geared box and the benefits from using it intelligently are really outstanding. For those who appreciate gearbox ratios, a study of the figures given in the accompanying panel will be most illuminating, for they are virtually to sports/racing motorcycle standards.

Coupled to this best of all gearboxes is an engine that thrives on r.p.m. When you first start it up and let it idle it sounds like a bucket of old nails, and is noisy compared with many 6-cylinder engines, but touch the throttle pedal and the rattling and clanking immediately turn into a whine that soon becomes a hum. Accelerating really hard up the rev. range in the gears you can't help being impressed by the way the engine becomes more like a dynamo the higher the r.p.m. go. Peak power is developed at 6,100 r.p.m., but 6,800 r.p.m. is permissible in the gears, though it is pointless to go so high in 1st or 2nd. Like all Porsches there is no hope of over-revving in top gear, for the Zuffenhausen engineers believe in high gearing and a close-ratio gearbox, a principle with which everyone who enjoys real motoring must agree. You can wind the 911 up to 6,800 r.p.m. in 4th gear and it will then comfortably reach 6,000 r.p.m. in 5th, which is a pretty honest 120 m.p.h. After that the revs take some time to build up higher, 6,200 often being seen, but 6,400 needing a Motorway. At that you are doing close on 130 m.p.h., which is not bad going for a fully equipped 2-litre car. Once there you feel you could hold it flat-out for ever, for the engine is so smooth and it seems to thrive on such r.p.m., unlike many other engines which get rough or fussy when they are on peak power. The old 1,600-c.c. Porsche 4-cylinder engines had exactly the same feeling about them, showing no signs of stress at peak power r.p.m. in top gear, and my old 1600 Super did many miles at 5,200 r.p.m. on full throttle in top gear. With the 911 even at Porsche's hoped-for maximum of 6,500 r.p.m. in 5th gear you still have 300 r.p.m. in hand before you reach the red line on the tachometer, and this gives a wonderful feeling of confidence, which I know from 10 years of Porsche driving to be justifiable confidence.

Like all Porsches, the 911 likes to be driven hard with the driver using the tachometer intelligently, and for this reason this instrument takes pride of place in the centre of the instrument panel, the two-pronged steering wheel giving a clear and unobstructed view of the 8,000 r.p.m. dial. Slightly to the right is the 150-m.p.h. speedometer, with mileage and trip recording, but this is rather a vaguely annotated dial, with markings at every 15 m.p.h. and figures only at 30, 60, 90, 120 and 150, so that by the time you have tried to decide what m.p.h. it is indicating you are probably doing some other speed. The fact that the speedo. is vaguely marked, smaller in diameter than the tachometer, and off to the right, rather indicates that Porsche do not intend it to be taken very seriously and it is there merely to comply with the law. The tachometer is the instrument to be used. After all, the 911 feels so safe and sure at any speed that mere m.p.h. becomes purely academic or legal, you drive the car at a speed commensurate with road conditions, for you know that it can use any road to the road's maximum capability.

The other instruments include a large-dial electric clock on the far right, with an adjustable red pointer for keeping a note of starting time, or appointment time, and on the left of the central tachometer are two combined instruments. The first tells you all you want to know about the condition of the oil in the dry sump lubrication system and the second tells you the quantities of liquids contained in the Porsche. The first dial has temperature in degrees-F. on one side and pressure in lb./sq. in. on the right. When under full sail, with everything functioning normally, the pressure is 80 lb./sq. in. and the temperature is 175° F. The second dial shows on one side fuel tank contents which says vaguely that you have 2/4 for half a tank, or 4/4 for a full tank. There is a red light indicating about 1¼ gallons as a reserve, but I feel it is a pity that the old foolproof three-position tap has been dropped, but this is due to a complete revision of the fuel tank and system, as will be explained later. On the other side of this second dial is a clever little indicator that shows you how much oil you have in the dry-sump oil tank. With the engine warm (at least 140° F.) and after idling for a little while, the needle will settle down and indicate the contents in the tank in litres, six litres being adequate, four litres being too low. Just in case you have no faith in electrics, there is a conventional dipstick in the oil tank, which is mounted on the right of the engine compartment.

While on cockpit equipment it is worth mentioning that there is the usual sort of key-starter, and the engine never seems to fire until you have let go of the key (voltage drop ?), a two-position lights switch, for sidelamps and headlamps, and this knob also controls a panel light rheostat, but it unfortunately does not extinguish the panel lights completely. Behind the steering wheel are two column-stalks, the right-hand one moving up and down parallel to the wheel rim for operating direction indicators, pulling backwards against a spring for headlamp flashers, and clicking from the neutral position away from you for full-beam headlamps. This arrangement is very good, for it means that when on dipped lamps no matter which way you move the lever in the heat of the moment you get full beam, which is often essential when travelling fast at night. The left-hand stalk controls wipers and washers, the wipers having a 3-speed motor operated by moving the stalk downwards in the plane of the steering wheel, while pulling the stalk towards you operates the washers. The heating and ventilation systems have a number of controls and ringing the changes on these can produce almost any desired condition. Just in front of the gear-lever is a short lever controlling the flow from the heater; pulling it rearwards closes air gates, by cables, which deflect hot air from the engine along the chassis members and into the car through vents just in front of the seats and through vents on the scuttle at the foot of the windscreen. The floor vents have sliding gates to control the flow, and a control on the scuttle opens a fresh-air vent in front of the windscreen which lets air into the base of the screen, along with the hot air. The rear quarter-light windows hinge open and their use is essential for ensuring a good flow of air, while the porous roof lining lets hot air pass out through vents across the top of the rear window, this large expanse of glass being warmed by air pipes from the main heating system. By juggling with the volume of heat from the centre control, the amount you let in from the floor vent, the opening of the rear quarter-lights and the fresh-air vent on the scuttle, you can get a very comfortable situation of being warm around the lower portions, while having cool fresh air on your face. The quantity of heat sent in from the engine cooling system is quite remarkable, and when travelling really fast you could easily suffer from scorched ankles! But to return to road driving again, for that is what the 911 is built for.

Forward visibility is outstanding, for the falling front gives a completely unobstructed view of the road, while visibility through the back and across the rear quarters is also very good for manoeuvring, the only criticism being the messy quarters around the windscreen pillars. Small swivelling panels are provided at the front of the side windows, and these make the windscreen pillars a bit thick, as well as having another vertical pillar in your line of vision when looking outwards for three-quarter forward vision, and pedestrians and cyclists can easily be lost in this area. Personally, I can find no use whatsoever for swivelling panels in the side windows, never having had them on my old Porsche, nor having them on my present E-type Jaguar. Apart from reducing three-quarter forward vision their only use seems to be to cause cold air currents on the passenger's legs, and for the driver to throw cigarette ends into the faces of overtaking motorcyclists. The seats are well up to Porsche standards, and have adjustment from the vertical to the horizontal for the squab, effected by a small lever at the base of the seat, while they have the normal fore and aft movement. Behind the front seats is a large luggage area, which lifts up in two halves to reveal small seats for the occasional, short-duration journey by short-stature passengers. With the large sloping rear window extending well forward along the roof, sitting in these rear seats seems very exposed, the glass being almost overhead. Night driving is very satisfactory, the lights being good for 120 m.p.h. on known roads, while 110-m.p.h. cruising in the dark on motorways is very relaxed. The headlamp full-beam indicator] is nicely subdued, as is the turn-indicator warning light.

When you visit the Porsche factory in Stuttgart you are more than likely to see Dr. Ferry Porsche arrive in one of his latest models, for he not only designs Porsche cars, but uses them as well, while Huscke von Hanstein, the Racing Manager, covers great mileages all over Europe in Porsches. If you go to Le Mans or the Targa Florio you will find members of the technical department in production Porsches as well as experimental ones, and because the people at Porsches use Porsche cars the customer gets the benefit of this in great attention to detail from the user point of view. In some makes of car you wonder whether the chief engineer or the managing director has ever driven them at all, but with Porsche it is the opposite. On the 911 there are three typical examples that immediately spring to mind. When the radio aerial is retracted it goes in flush with its base and can only be withdrawn again by means of a small key-cum-hook attached to the ignition key. This may seem a strange thing to do, but if you have had your aerial pulled up and then bent at right-angles by French or Italian hooligans, as I have, while the car is parked outside a hotel at night, you will appreciate this feature. The fuel filler is concealed beneath a flap on the top of the left-hand wing in front of the windscreen, this flap being opened by a release knob and cable on the instrument panel. Inside this recess is a rubber apron that has to be unfolded before the tank cap is revealed, the apron then lying over the edge of the aperture guarding the paintwork of the body against clumsy petrol pump attendants who knock chips of paint off with the hose nozzle, while it also catches the inevitable drips. The third detail is the provision of two lights in the front luggage locker that light up when the lid is raised. These sort of details, so typical in the 911, come from usage by members of the factory staff with real motoring experience. Similar things are the provision of coat hooks behind the seats, a safety catch on the passenger seat to prevent it pitching forward under heavy braking when it is unoccupied, clips to retain the hinged rear seat-backs when they are unoccupied, a funnel in

Instrument layout. The rev.-counter by its size and position is the most important instrument, as, of course, it should be in a GT car.

the neck of the windscreen washer bag to facilitate filling, the provision of a rubber bag for the washer fluid and, not a glass bottle like some people still fit, push-button interior operation for the doors instead of levers, anti-dazzle rear-view mirror, a towing hook built into the front of the chassis, useful map pockets in the doors and on the sides of the bulkhead, and a simple white light in the oil gauge's dial to show that the hand-brake is on when the ignition is switched on.

The lid of the engine compartment is opened by a knob recessed into the left-hand door pillar, concealed when the door is closed, and the front luggage compartment lid is released by a knob under the instrument panel. Both lids are self-supporting, controlled by pneumatic dampers to stay in any position. The front luggage compartment is very much larger than on earlier Porsches and presents a useful carpeted space into which small objects can be put without being lost. This is achieved by mounting the spare wheel flat in the bottom of the nose, and building a shaped petrol tank that surrounds the spare wheel, the 12-volt battery taking up one corner of this area. In spite of the tank filler neck having to run upwards through some curves to the wing flap it is possible to put full petrol pump pressure into the filler without any blow-back occurring. It is this low mounting of the fuel tank that prevents the use of the old Porsche/VW type of reserve petrol tap, for the tank lies well below the level of the carburetters and a Bendix electric pump sucks the petrol to the rear of the car.

Carburation on the 6-cylinder engine is by a series of three Solex carburetters to each bank of cylinders, and these operate on the "weir" fuel feed system. The Bendix pump feeds a collector box below each trio of carburetters, from whence a pipe-line runs to a mechanical pump that feeds a gallery running along the level of each trio of chokes. The jets take what fuel they require and the surplus drains down into the collector boxes, there being a mechanical pump for each row of carburetters, these pumps being driven off the rear of the left-hand camshaft. In accordance with new American constructional regulations the engine and oil tank breathers are fed into the carburetter intake filters, which is all very well, but if the oil tank is inadvertently overfilled and frothing occurs it can cause oil mist to pass through the engine, so that quite a cloud of blue smoke will come out of the single, large-diameter exhaust pipe when starting up. In case oil should collect in the main air-filter body there is a drain pipe to lead it away into the nether regions of the gearbox, but during the test this little rubber pipe fell off. Due to some misinformation I overfilled the oil tank, with the consequence that an ominous layer of oil began to appear on top of the engine, but A.F.N. Ltd. soon solved this problem for me.

As will have been gathered by now, the new Porsche 911 is a most interesting car technically and is one that is a real joy to drive. Its first-class stability, hard-working engine, perfect gearbox, accurate steering, high cornering propensities, and one-piece feel make it a real GT car, a car that is intended for hard motoring. The harder you drive it the more it seems to come alive, and you can almost hear it chuckling to itself as you really begin to use it the way Dr. Porsche meant it to be used. No matter what you do it never seems to become embarrassed, like many so-called GT cars, and I imagine it would be terrific on a journey through rugged mountain country (perhaps I can borrow one for this year's trip to Sicily). It has all the creature comforts desirable for long journeys, is a 2-seater with plenty of luggage room, and tiny occasional seats for giving a lift to the inevitable third person; in fact, all the attributes that go to make a real GT car. Above all else it is a car that makes it very clear that it enjoys being driven hard and fast, and it is with you all the way through thick and thin; an incredibly safe car that you know you can trust, and if you make a mistake when driving it fast it will stay with you and help you to sort things out, in true Porsche fashion, and not give up and embarrass you at an inopportune moment, like some well-known cars.

Now if Dr. Porsche could find some way of getting the power and torque of a 4.2-litre Jaguar engine into the 911 we would have something approaching the perfect GT car. As it is, Porsche have made an outstanding car in the 911, that carries on from where the old 2-litre Carrera left off, and it sets standards towards which everyone should endeavour to arrive. Needless to say nothing is perfect and there are probably things about the 911 which would upset and annoy many people, such as the engine noise at tickover, or the wind noise at 100 m.p.h., or the fact that it doesn't have a boot like a Ford Zephyr, or that it doesn't have an automatic gearbox, and no doubt many professional road testers will write sneering remarks about the shortcomings of the 911. If they do then all I can say is that they can't be capable of enjoying motoring with a capital M, motoring for the sheer fun of handling a good car. The Porsche 911 is such terrific fun to drive fast that if you cannot forgive it a few defects then you don't deserve to be driving it and you should be in a "Crootmobile" or some other family saloon.

During the test period the British Drag Racing Association were holding a practice meeting on the standing-start ¼-mile, so I took the opportunity of pitting the 911 against the electronic-beam timers, and it recorded a best time of 15.62 sec., with numerous runs just under 16 sec. A driver completely strange to the car also got under 16 sec. on his first attempt. For the quarter-mile it was only necessary to use 1st, 2nd and 3rd gears, the finishing line being crossed at 6,800 r.p.m. in 3rd gear, a speed of approximately 92 m.p.h.—and there remained the nice thought that there were still two more gears to come!

As with most good things there is always a snag, and with the 911 it is the price, which is in Britain of £3,438 1s. 3d., which includes purchase tax, import duty, and all the other costs that are involved in importing cars from a foreign country. The lucky Germans can buy this splendid car for about the price we pay for an E-type Jaguar. Another small snag is the fuel consumption, especially for a 2-litre car, for it showed a little over 18 m.p.g. overall, while if you keep it above 6,500 all the time it will drop to nearly 16 m.p.g. However, I presume that if you can afford the total purchase price you are not very worried about fuel consumption, and if you enjoy motoring and value things as a ratio of enjoyment/consumption/cost, then the 911 comes out very high. After a glorious week with the 911 Porsche I rate it as one of the great cars of today by all standards.

THE PORSCHE TYPE 911/2000

Engine: Six cylinders, horizontally opposed, 80 × 66 mm. (1,991 c.c.). Inclined overhead valves operated by overhead camshafts and rockers on each bank of cylinders. Camshafts chain driven. 9-to-1 c.r., 130 (DIN) b.h.p. at 6,100 r.p.m. (148 S.A.E. b.h.p.). Dry sump lubrication.

Gear ratios: 1st, 2.833 to 1; 2nd, 1.778 to 1; 3rd, 1.217 to 1; 4th, 0.962 to 1; 5th, 0.821 to 1. Axle ratio: 7 to 31 (4.428 to 1).

Tyres: 165 HR15 SP Dunlop, on bolt-on steel disc wheels.

Weight: DIN kerb weight, 21.2 cwt. (manufacturer's figure).

Steering ratio: 1 to 16.5.

Fuel capacity: 13¾ gallons (Imperial).

Wheelbase: 7 ft. 3 in.

Track: Front, 4 ft. 4½ in.; rear, 4 ft. 3¾ in.

Dimensions: 13 ft. 8 in. × 5 ft. 3½ in. × 4 ft. 4 in. (high). Ground clearance: 5.9 in.

Price: £2,844 plus £594 1s. 3d. purchase tax—total U.K., £3,438 1s. 3d.

Makers: Dr. Ing.h.c. F. Porsche KG., Stuttgart-Zuffenhausen, W. Germany.

Concessionaires: Porsche Cars Great Britain Ltd. (late A.F.N. Ltd.).

CAR AND DRIVER ROAD TEST

PORSCHE 911 S

"This is no car for a novice," warns a Porsche brochure.
All told, the admonition is a bit gratuitous.

Oversteer is back—and Porsche's got it! Early Porsches had it too, and now it has come full circle. Barely three years ago, Porsche employed a device called a "camber compensator" to curb the oversteering tendencies of the 356 series. Then the completely redesigned suspension of the 911 and 912 models made Porsches behave like normal, front-engined cars, and the purists started to carp. Porsche had even hidden an iron weight behind the 912's front bumper to keep the back end from coming around. Sure, understeer is safe—great for the masses—but oversteer makes driving fun . . . if you're expert enough to handle it. Fanciers of the marque yearned for the good old days when they used to *wischen* their Speedsters through turns, tails all hung out, arms sawing away like mad on the steering wheel.

Porsche is making a car for these drivers again, offering a sportier version of the 6-cylinder 911 dubbed the 911S. S for Super. Super because horsepower is up 20%, from 148 to 180. Super because the brake discs are vented. And Super because the suspension has been modified with strengthened struts, Koni adjustable shocks, a stiffer front anti-sway bar, and an anti-sway bar added at the rear.

The rear anti-sway bar, in addition to reducing body lean, has an effect diametrically opposed to that of the old "camber compensator." *Gott im Himmel! Übersteuer!* We'll hang out our tails on the Siegfried Line. "This is no car for a novice," warns a Porsche brochure.

The 911S's introduction has occasioned a shuffle in Porsche's marketing structure so that it now approximates the former ascending scale of Normal, Super and Carrera engines in the same body. The prices have been rearranged too. On the bottom

> For a 2-liter sports car,
> a quarter-mile in 15.2 sec.
> at 92 mph ranks with
> building a replica of
> the Great Pyramid
> of Cheops overnight.

rung is the 102-hp, 4-cylinder 912, with a base price of $4790, up $100 from last year, but two instrument panel gauges have been added. The 148-hp, 6-cylinder 911 is now $5990, *down* $500 from last year. However, many items that were standard on the 911 in '66 are optional in '67. In effect, it becomes simply a higher-powered version of the 912. The flagship of the fleet, the $6990, 180-hp, 6-cylinder 911S, is loaded with performance, luxury, and distinctive features like racy-looking forged magnesium-alloy wheels, a leather-covered steering wheel rim, extra instrumentation, an auxiliary gasoline heater, fog lights, pile carpets, and waffled padding on the dash. Most of these unique options are available—for a price—on the 911 and 912 (the mag wheels for $175), along with the old standbys like chromed steel road wheels.

In our zeal to obtain a 911S for a road test, we had to settle for one right off the boat. The car hadn't been dealer-prepared, much less fine-tuned, and it wasn't exactly in full song. Acceleration times were little better than those of a Weber-carbureted 911 5-speed we drove recently, which clocked 0-60 mph in 6.9 seconds and the standing quarter-mile in 15.6 seconds at 90 mph. Actually, our times were nearly identical to those claimed for the 911S by Porsche. The German government requires car manufacturers to certify performance which can be duplicated by any production model straight off the showroom floor. The factory figures are therefore ultra-conservative and represent the slowest car within assembly-line tolerances. Careful tuning of a 911S with some mileage on it should hack close to a second off our 0-60 mph time of 6.5 seconds. Still, neither that, nor a quarter-mile in 15.2 seconds at 92 mph (with three gears yet to go) is bad for *any* high-performance car. For a little 2-liter sports car, it ranks with Robert Moses building a replica of the Great Pyramid of Cheops overnight.

The brakes on our test car left something to be desired, although—again—were enormously above average. The 911 and 912 have Ate-Dunlop solid discs on all four wheels; the 911S's discs have internal radial venting. Vented discs are new to Porsche; so new, in fact, that Porsche has mistakenly laid claim to building the first sports car thus equipped. The Corvette Sting Ray has had vented discs since 1965, at which time Chevrolet claimed to be first with drums inside the rear discs for the parking/emergency brake. Porsche had had *that* feature since

> Within normal driving limits, and with reasonable caution, the 911S handles head and shoulders above practically everything else on the road.

1964, so perhaps the current German boast is just Porsche's way of getting back at Chevy.

At any rate, the bugs aren't yet out of Porsche's vented discs. True, they run cooler, making them less prone to fade, and lengthening pad life, but they are more difficult to modulate. If Ford's experience with vented discs on their Le Mans-winning Mk. II is any indication, the problem may be that the discs aren't dimensionally and/or geometrically stable. In our 80-0 mph braking test, the left rear wheel would invariably lock up, and the shortest stopping distance we could record was 271 ft. (.71G). Not half bad, but we knew the car could do better. Later, we sampled another 911S, and, after heating up the rather hard pads, it stopped from 80 mph in 242 ft. (.88G), but we have stopped a solid-disc 911 in 218 ft. (.98G), which is more like what the true potential is.

Normally, we measure a car's cornering power by clocking lap times on a skid pad of a known radius. We don't use an accelerometer, or Tapley meter, because it adds the vehicle's roll angle to the absolute lateral acceleration, and there is no accurate way to distinguish between the two. (Similarly, on braking and acceleration, the vehicle's pitch angle is automatically included in the reading.) However, during one phase of this test, we had the opportunity to ride shotgun with expert Porsche pilot Lake Underwood as he booted the 911S around a road circuit. Out of curiosity, we installed a lateral accelerometer to measure the 911S's cornering power. On level, unbanked turns, the instrument showed a maximum reading of .93G on right-hand corners, and .89G on left-hand bends. Subtracting a generous 9° (.10G) for roll angle, the 911S's limit of controllability is well over .81G.

The 911S's oversteer characteristic appears early in the car's cornering range. At low lateral accelerations, it understeers mildly. From .40G on up, less and less steering lock is

PORSCHE 911S

Importer: Porsche of America Corp.
107 Tryon Ave. West
Teaneck, N.J.

Number of dealers in U.S.: 244

Vehicle type: Rear-engine, rear-wheel-drive, 2+2-passenger GT car

Price as tested: $7,255 (Manufacturer's suggested retail price, plus Federal excise tax, dealer preparation and delivery charges; does not include state and local taxes, license or freight charges)

Options on test car: AM-FM radio ($180.00)

ENGINE
Type: Air-cooled flat six, aluminum block, 12-port aluminum heads, 8 main bearings
Bore x stroke......3.15 x 2.60 in, 80 x 66 mm
Displacement............121.5 cu in, 1991 cc
Compression ratio.......................9.8 to one
Carburetion....... 2 x 3-bbl Weber 46 IDA 3Cs
Valve gear..........Single overhead camshafts on each bank, chain-driven, rocker arms
Power (SAE)............180 bhp @ 6600 rpm
Torque (SAE)........144 lbs/ft @ 5200 rpm
Specific power output..........1.48 bhp/cu in, 90.5 bhp/liter
Max. recommended engine speed...7200 rpm

DRIVE TRAIN
Transmission:....5-speed manual, all-synchro
Clutch diameter.........................8.46 in
Final drive ratio........................4.43 to one

Gear	Ratio	Mph/1000 rpm	Max. test speed
I	3.09	5.3	38 mph (7200 rpm)
II	1.89	8.8	63 mph (7200 rpm)
III	1.32	12.5	89 mph (7200 rpm)
IV	1.04	15.9	114 mph (7200 rpm)
V	0.79	20.9	140 mph (6700 rpm)

DIMENSIONS AND CAPACITIES
Wheelbase.................................87.1 in
Track...................F:53.4 in, R:52.2 in
Length...................................163.9 in
Width.....................................63.4 in
Height....................................52.0 in
Ground clearance..........................5.9 in
Curb weight..............................2279 lbs
Test weight..............................2535 lbs
Weight distribution, F/R.............41/59%
Lbs/bhp (test weight).....................14.0
Battery capacity..........12 volts, 45 amp/hr
Alternator capacity...................420 watts
Fuel capacity............................16.4 gal
Oil capacity..............................9.5 qts

SUSPENSION
F: Ind., MacPherson strut with lower wishbone, longitudinal torsion bars, anti-sway bar, Koni adjustable shock absorbers
R: Ind., semi-trailing links, transverse torsion bars, anti-sway bar, Koni adjustable shock absorbers

STEERING
Type......................Rack and pinion
Turns lock-to-lock.........................2.75
Turning circle.............................34 ft

BRAKES
F: Ate-Dunlop 11.1-in. vented discs
R: Ate-Dunlop 11.25-in. vented discs with integral 7.09-in. drums for handbrake
Swept area........................371.0 sq in

WHEELS AND TIRES
Wheel size and type: ....4.5J x 15-in, aluminum alloy, 5-bolt
Tire make, size and type..Dunlop HR 165-15 SP radial-ply, tube-type
Test inflation pressures...F: 32 psi, R: 35 psi
Tire load rating: .....810 lbs per tire @ 24 psi

PERFORMANCE
Zero to	Seconds
30 mph	2.2
40 mph	3.4
50 mph	4.8
60 mph	6.5
70 mph	9.0
80 mph	11.4
90 mph	14.6
100 mph	18.2

Standing ¼-mile...........15.2 sec @ 92 mph
80-0 mph............................271 ft (.71 G)
Fuel mileage......14-18 mpg on premium fuel
Cruising range ....230-296 m

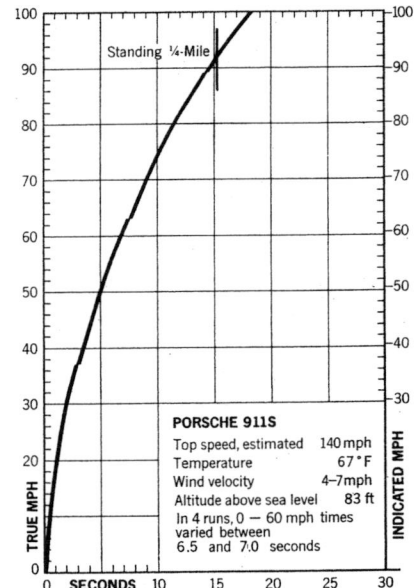

PORSCHE 911S
Top speed, estimated 140 mph
Temperature 67°F
Wind velocity 4-7mph
Altitude above sea level 83 ft
In 4 runs, 0 — 60 mph times varied between 6.5 and 7.0 seconds

CHECK LIST

ENGINE
Starting.............................Fair
Response.........................Excellent
Vibration.........................Excellent
Noise...............................Fair

DRIVE TRAIN
Shift linkage....................Very Good
Synchro action..................Excellent
Clutch smoothness..............Excellent
Transmission noise...............Excellent

STEERING
Effort............................Very Good
Response.........................Excellent
Road feel........................Excellent
Kickback........................Very Good

SUSPENSION
Ride comfort.........................Good
Roll resistance...................Very Good
Pitch control....................Very Good
Harshness control....................Good

HANDLING
Directional control..............Very Good
Predictability...................Very Good
Evasive maneuverability..........Excellent
Resistance to sidewinds..............Fair

BRAKES
Pedal pressure...................Very Good
Response.........................Excellent
Fade resistance..................Excellent
Directional control..............Excellent

CONTROLS
Wheel position...................Excellent
Pedal position...................Very Good
Gearshift position...................Good
Relationship.....................Excellent
Small controls.......................Good

INTERIOR
Ease of entry/exit...................Good
Noise level (cruising)...............Good
Front seating comfort............Excellent
Front leg room...................Excellent
Front head room.................Very Good
Front hip/shoulder room..............Good
Rear seating comfort.................Poor
Rear leg room........................Poor
Rear head room......................Poor
Rear hip/shoulder room..............Poor
Instrument comprehensiveness....Excellent
Instrument legibility............Excellent

VISION
Forward..........................Excellent
Front quarter....................Very Good
Side.............................Excellent
Rear quarter.........................Fair
Rear................................Fair

WEATHER PROTECTION
Heater/defroster.................Excellent
Ventilation.........................Fair
Weather sealing..................Very Good

CONSTRUCTION QUALITY
Sheet metal......................Excellent
Paint............................Excellent
Chrome...........................Very Good
Upholstery.......................Excellent
Padding..........................Very Good
Hardware.........................Very Good

GENERAL
Headlight illumination...............Good
Parking and signal lights........Excellent
Wiper effectiveness..............Very Good
Service accessibility................Fair
Trunk space..........................Fair
Interior storage space...............Good
Bumper protection....................Fair

PORSCHE 911S

needed to keep this car on a given course. By .70G, it's in a full-blooded four-wheel drift, and the steering behavior is back-tracking toward neutral-steer. Beyond the limit of the tires' rolling adhesion, the 911S reacts like any car with a rearward weight bias, and spins, or, if you're quick enough to catch it, powerslides like an old dirt-track roadster. All told, Porsche's admonition, "not for the novice" is a bit gratuitous. Within normal driving limits and with reasonable caution, the 911S handles predictably, controllably, and head and shoulders above practically anything else on the road.

There's always room for improvement, however, and the present limitations on the 911S's absolute cornering power are imposed by its wheels and tires. We were stunned to learn that the rim width of those flashy new wheels is still only 4½ inches, a mere half-inch wider than a Volkswagen's, and unchanged since Porsche went from 16-in. to 15-in. wheels in the dim dawn of time. Four-and-a-half inches was unfashionably skinny even then, and is almost inconceivable today. Porsche ballyhoos the notion that their racing program improves the breed of their production cars, but the competition-bred lesson of the benefits of wide-rim wheels has apparently gone unheeded. One-inch wider rims alone would have wrought as much improvement in the car's handling ability as all their tricks with rear anti-sway bars, stiffer shocks and spring rates, and radial-ply tires. Wide-rim racing wheels are available from Porsche for competition drivers, and American Racing Equipment in San Francisco is doing a land-office business in 5- and 6-in. mag wheels for disc-braked Porsches. The introduction of Porsche's own mag wheel would have been an ideal opportunity to cash in on the trend, but Stuttgart fumbled the ball. We can only surmise that steps will soon be taken to correct this state of affairs. In the meantime, it is of some consolation that the new wheels aid brake heat dissipation and reduce unsprung weight.

The 911S's radial-ply tires, German Dunlop SPs, are the other limiting factor. Radial-ply tires are generally advantageous, developing a higher cornering force at a lower slip angle than conventional tires. They do this by keeping more rubber on the road through a softer lateral compliance—the tread stays flat on the ground while the sidewall rolls. This gives radials an odd feel; they mush sideways until the slack is taken up, then they grip. The SPs, in particular, have an odd tread pattern, like a knobby snow tire, with S-shaped cleats and a deep (¼-inch) tread depth. The cleats are so tall that they bend like willows under side loads. Coupled with the normal mushiness of radials, the SPs give a sensation somewhat akin to riding on bristles. It would be interesting to try a 911S with a shallow-tread radial-ply tire, like the Michelin X, or an American high-performance tire, like the Firestone Wide Oval.

The only real handling *fault* of the 911S is a corkscrewing motion of the front end when cornering on an undulating surface. This appears to be a by-product of the Porsche's unconventional MacPherson strut front suspension. There is no loss of adhesion or directional stability, but with a lack of other vices it stood out disconcertingly.

If we've dwelled on the 911S's handling traits, it's because they are the most obvious departure from the standard 911, impressing us far more than the 32 extra horsepower. The 180-hp engine is notable mainly for its lack of temperament. Its idle is slightly more uneven, it accelerates with a more vigorous growl, prefers super-premium fuel, and consumes it a shade more prodigally than the 911. The power and torque curves aren't "peaky," and, except for an ill-advised change in gearing, it pulls as well from low revs. Revving it beyond its 7200 rpm redline would be all too easy were it not for a centrifugal ignition governor concealed in the distributor arm.

With racing versions of Porsche's flat-six pulling close to 235 horsepower, raising the output of the street engine to 180 horsepower was easy—a matter of subtle changes in the cam timing and carburetor jetting (Webers are used on all 6-cylinder Porsches now), plus an increase in compression ratio from 9.0- to 9.8-to-one. Initial reports indicate that there is less carbon build-up with the higher compression ratio. Oil control appears to be difficult even on the 148-hp engine, however, with most owners reporting 400-500 miles per quart. The dry sump holds nearly two gallons, so topping up could be a matter of every other gas stop.

The original 911 had a long, 2.83 first gear, which made the car hard to start from rest. To ease the load on the clutch, first gear on all Porsches has been shortened to 3.09, with the other gears closed up in suit. The 911 and 912 have .86 high gears while the 911S has a .79 high gear, enabling its engine to wind the car out to its full top-speed potential of 140 mph. Unfortunately, this has resulted in a wider gap between fourth and fifth gears, and a 20% loss of pulling power in high. A gearchange is necessary for surprisingly mild hills. Since nobody in his right mind should think the unthinkable—140 mph on our public highways—a shorter fifth gear would mean less rowing back-and-forth on the gearshift lever. We really didn't mind more frequent use of the transmission, though; slicing through the Porsche's gears remains one of the great delights of the Western Hemisphere.

Little else is changed from the 911 of our April, 1965 Road Research Report. The styling still looks good to us, and, like any Porsche, it has personality in its design, workmanship, and its seat-of-the-pants telegraphy about what it's doing. The firmer ride heightens this sensation, although thankfully, the increase in stiffness has not been accompanied by a similar increase in harshness. Sidewind sensitivity, already a tender subject with 911 owners, is, if anything, slightly worse in the 911S, although hardly noticeable below a thoroughly illegal 120 mph.

Maybe it's just us, but, in retrospect, the steering wheel seems oversized, giving more leverage than needed on one of the easiest-steering cars built today. Also, we note that an optional spacer can bring the wheel 1½-inches closer to the driver, which we think we'd prefer. Otherwise, the interior is a model for the way all cars should be built—sports cars or utility sedans, front-engined or rear, Detroit or Kharkov. The seats, upholstered in a new air-flow weaving, stay cooler, and, as always, are almost infinitely adjustable to a variety of comfortable positions. There's plenty of room (except, perhaps, elbow room), and all the controls are located where you can get at them easily and operate them efficiently.

Just cruising around town or belting along back roads like a would-be racer, the 911S is a great way for getting from Point A to Point B, even when Point B represented only an excuse to drive somewhere.

Each successive Porsche has been the ultimate Porsche, which is akin to its being the ultimate luxury GT car. The 911S surely must be the all-time high. Where can Porsche go from here? Build a car with disappearing headlights?

Driving Impression of the
PORSCHE 911S

IF THERE'S ANYTHING I don't like, it's an article about a car which starts right off saying that the machine being evaluated is one of the greatest current creations of the automotive genus before the reader can judge the report for himself. So I won't say that about the Porsche 911S. I'd like to, but I won't.

The 911S represents the latest thinking of Stuttgart Porschewerk No. 2 (No. 1 is the prototype racing department), and the one I drove was the only Porsche I've seen done up completely in black, inside and out. The 911S looks almost exactly like the 911, being built up from the same basic chassis and body on the same assembly line.

There are several external differences, however. One is the golden "S" next to the 911 badge on the engine lid, another is a large rubber insert in the wrap-around bumpers, and the third, by far the most noticeable, is the set of magnesium alloy wheels.

The cockpit is virtually perfect. The entire dash is done in walnut and leatherette, with all instruments properly placed and easily readable, including one which tells you exactly how much oil you have in the crankcase. The steering wheel is just the right size and leather covered. The seats are extremely comfortable and cradle the occupants properly for long trips and hard cornering.

The 911S buyer has a choice of upholstery: all leather, leatherette-corduroy, or leatherette-wool black-and-white dogtooth combination. I had the latter, and though ambient temperatures got up to nearly 80, it never became uncomfortable. One reason for this was the ventilation system, which sends an even flow of fresh air throughout the interior at all road speeds. In addition, my car was fitted with an electrically operated sunroof, an extra option which I heartily recommend. It makes it possible to air out the cockpit instantly without blowing everything out an open window at 100 mph.

There's an upholstered fold-down shelf in the rear for luggage. When up it reveals two neat bucket seats for occasional adult use which are really meant for kids. The whole car is full of goodies like 3-speed electric windscreen wipers and washers, interior operated gas filler lock, steering-column-mounted high-low dimmer, flasher, horn, turn signals, all perfectly laid out, a self-finding radio which operates on five bands, full interior carpeting, adjustable rear seat heating, a rear window windshield-wiper (optional), full shoulder harness, vanity mirrors on the rear of the padded sun visors, and so on and on.

All this can be matched on the 911, including the mag wheels, by adding the few things which are missing as optional equipment. Neither is the engine compartment basically different. It simply has its teeth full of two upright Weber 3-throat carburetors instead of the 911's two Solexes. The suspension has a few additions, namely a double rear stabilizer bar as well as a reinforced front one. You can have them put on a 911 too. In fact, when you come right down to it, the 911S is basically the 911 with all the extras already on it.

To drive any of the 900 family is a thing of beauty and a joy forever, but the 6-cyl 911S, with the added punch of the Webers, which deliver about 20% more hp than the Solexes, is really a satisfying experience.

The 5-speed gearbox has a very short throw, about an inch over and half an inch back—or so it feels—to hook into first. The car starts off very smoothly, very silently, and the next thing you know, it's going 5500 rpm and time to get out of first. In goes the clutch, and the barest touch on the gearshift is enough to make it pop out of first and move almost automatically into second. The first time this happens you get nervous, thinking it can't really be all that secure in first if all it takes is a nudge to get it out. But it is.

The rest of the gears are about eight inches apart at the gearshift knob level—which is a trifle long for my taste, because it brings the handle back almost to sidepocket level in third or fifth. However, within several miles I got used to this and paid no attention to it any longer.

The car handles so smoothly that in city driving it is very difficult to stay under 40 mph. It just wants to go that fast, slipping in and out of traffic, making virtually no apparent noise (due in part to the excellent cockpit insulation), and still in second, or, at best, third. In Germany at least, nobody, except an occasional huge Mercedes, will argue right of way with a new model Porsche.

THERE was a time when the critic's description of the Porsche as a go-faster version of the Volkswagen had a grain of truth in it. Both cars, the prosaic bread-and-butter family saloon, dull and solid and well-finished and efficient, and the svelte GT coupés with their high performance, exciting handling and quality image had a common pedigree. The original Porsche, the project 356, was developed directly from the early post-war Volkswagens by Ferry Porsche, son of Professor Ferdinand Porsche who had designed the original VW and who was then held in a French prison until the million-mark ransom demanded by the authorities could be raised. The idea was to use the best of the raw material of the VW as a basis for a high-performance two-seater coupé which would attack the prestige market in a way which the humble VW could never hope to. The efficient and reliable VW flat-four air-cooled engine was developed to give more power, the suspension settings were changed to give tauter handling at fast speed, and the mechanicals were enclosed in a more streamlined body which was designed to save weight as well as air resistance.

But ever since then the Porsches have been climbing further and further away from their humble origins. Detail developments and improvements to Porsche and VW have led both cars along different routes, until now they are distant relatives at best. And three years ago, Porsche severed one of the last links in the chain by introducing two completely new models, with a body-chassis combination which was very different from the old. One of these cars, the 912, still used the latest version of the flat four-cylinder engine developed all the way from the original VW unit, while the other model, the 911, broke new ground by using the six-cylinder

Handsome is as handsome does—the fast and attractive Porsche 911S qualifies on both counts.

horizontally-opposed overhead-camshaft (one per bank) dry-sump engine developed from the power units used in the Porsche racing cars. And last year Porsche announced a still hotter version of this car, using the same two-litre six, but modified to give 160 bhp at peak instead of 130, giving the car a top speed of around 140 mph and an acceleration which pushed it to 60 mph in just eight seconds from a standing start.

Driving a Porsche—any Porsche—is the kind of experience every car enthusiast should have at least once in his lifetime. Porsche fanatics have an intense loyalty to the *marque* which isn't always easy for outsiders to appreciate, until they try the cars for themselves. The combination of smooth and effortless acceleration (probably the best single safety measure of all, whatever the self-styled experts may say) aided by a five-speed gearbox which is still the standard by which all the others are judged, and a very free-revving engine adds up to a kind of driving all too different from the type most of us have to endure all too often. Traffic, poor road surfaces, congestion and long distances all lose their terrors—in a car as comfortable and obedient as this. The excellent seats, the light steering, the siting of the controls and the high standard of finish both inside and outside back up the inherently safe handilng to produce a car which is a rare joy to drive.

Probably the most attractive feature of the car is the evidence of the careful thought which has gone into the minor details. The petrol filler cap which can only be released from inside the car and which contains a special pad to protect the bodywork from spillage, the *three* speed windscreen wipers with *four*-jet washers, the electric clock with the time-of-travel hand, the ignition cut-out which prevents you from exceeding 7300 rpm, the oil-level indicator. Of course there are disadvantages—no car ever made has been perfect—rear seat passengers are short on access and headroom, engine noise is fairly high and the wheels can be spun on wet roads—but match these niggles against the solid advantages, and it's obvious Porsche have their priorities right. Superb value for money—even at £3557!

PORSCHE 911 S

Is this the most desirable Porsche yet?

Sporting Motorist's Test Team put the 911S through its paces to find out

the answers to this and other pertinent questions

Think twice before you road test a Porsche.

A Porsche is so responsive to your touch, it seems to read your mind. You can almost *think* it through a turn. It drives the way you feel like driving: calmly competent on the way to work, razor-sharp and aggressive on racing weekends. Whatever your mood, this car instinctively matches it. (One of the enduring pleasures of owning a Porsche.)

Racing's toughest competition car never fights its driver

The Porsche is a well-mannered champion —an honor graduate of the world's most unforgiving obedience courses: LeMans, Targa Florio, Sebring, Nurburgring. It has won the World Cup for Speed and Endurance, awarded by the sponsors of these four races.

The Porsche will corner safely, on virtually any line you choose. The suspension (independent torsion bars and trailing arms) and the car's superb balance keep the wheels always pressed, full tread, against the road. On unpaved streets or rough, back-country washboards, the suspension eliminates rebounds and kidney jolts. The steering (via fast rack-and-pinion linkage) always responds faithfully to your touch.

Shifting gears is effortless. As quickly as you can move your arm, you can shift up or down, for maximum engine efficiency.

And reassuringly, the Porsche is as obedient when you want to stop as it is when you want to go. All four wheels are equipped with fade-proof, self-adjusting disc brakes, built to take the most destructive handling professional racing drivers can give them. An impressive margin of safety for everyday street driving.

The sincerest form of flattery

Porsche's formidable racing record is reason enough to get acquainted with this car. So is Porsche's automotive history.

The man behind this car, Professor Ferdinand Porsche, patented the first torsion bar suspension and pioneered the aerodynamic fastback. He mounted his cars' engines in the rear (all *grand prix* racing cars today have rear-mounted engines). He developed a lightweight, air-cooled engine that's almost indestructible.

The creative tradition established by Professor Porsche is clearly evident in the work of his son and grandsons. Case in point: their new roll-bar-equipped Targa convertible. (Some day, all convertibles may offer the Porsche Targa's built-in safety feature.)

When you road test a Porsche, you'll discover how comfortable it

PORSCHE 911 S

HANDLING
Rear-engined cars are often said to suffer from chronic oversteer. If so, then the Porsche must be the exception which proves the rule. The small, neat leather-covered steering wheel controls a car which feels very well-balanced indeed. At first the car tends to understeer, but this tendency is only a slight one, giving way quickly to completely neutral handling even over wicked surfaces and on the tightest of bends. The powerful engine and the well-spaced ratios in the gearbox allow the driver to bring the tail of the car round as and when he wishes—but there is very little body roll,

SEATING
Seats upholstered in leatherette. Front seats adjustable for rake and fore-and-aft movement.
Front seat legroom: 18-28 ins.
Front seat headroom: 38 ins.
Distance to pedals: 13-23 ins.

STEERING
ZF rack and pinion steering. 2.7 turns from lock-to-lock giving a turning circle of 32-34 ft between kerbs.

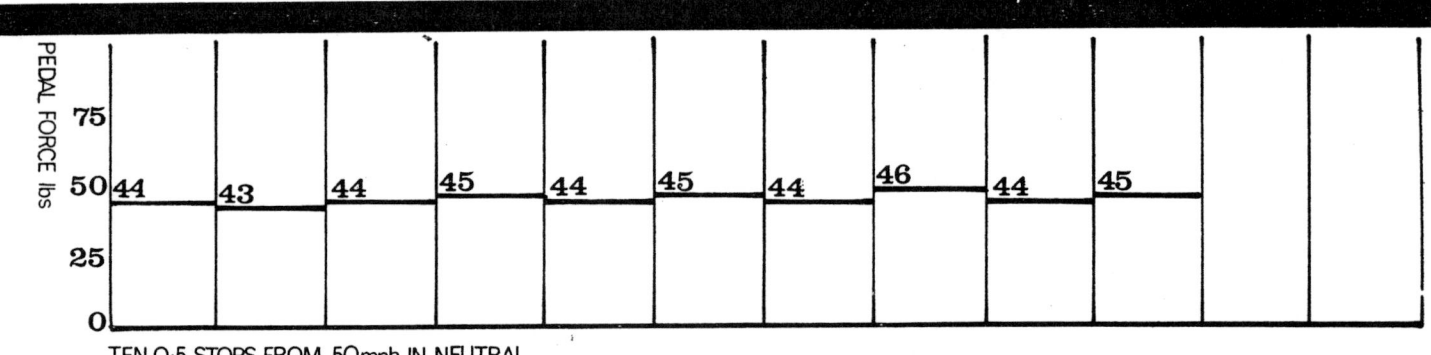

TEN 0·5 STOPS FROM 50mph IN NEUTRAL

ENGINE AND MECHANICAL DATA
Engine
Six-cylinder: horizontally opposed single overhead camshaft (for each bank of cylinders) air-cooled unit of 1991 cc capacity. Bore: 80 mm. Stroke: 66 mm. Compression ratio: 9.8 to one. Carburation: 2 Weber 40 IDA 3C. The engine develops maximum power of 160 bhp at 6600 rpm and maximum torque of 132 lb ft at 5200 rpm.

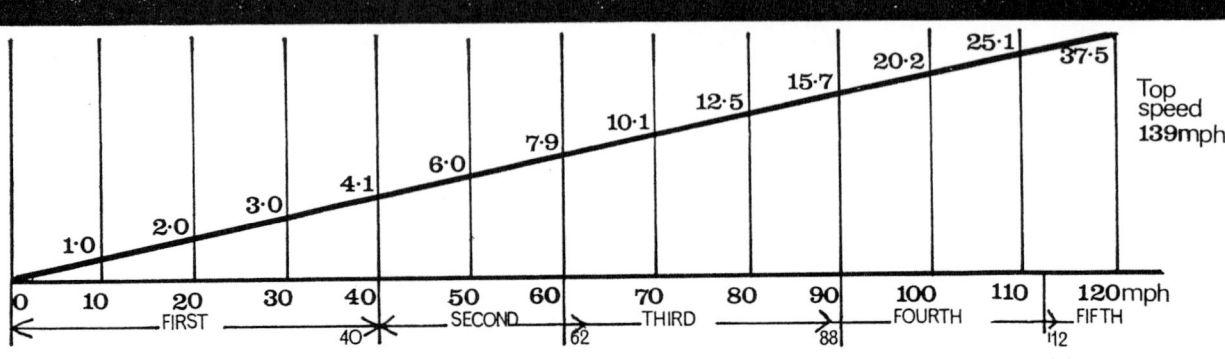

and the car never produces anything unexpected or undesirable.

With such a high standard of roadholding, most people would expect a stiff ride. In fact, the ride is only choppy at low speeds—once the car is moving at the kinds of speeds for which it was designed, the suspension takes bumps and surface irregularities in its stride. The front seats are well-shaped and locate driver and passenger as well as supporting them.

Part of the ease of the car's handling comes from the superb Porsche gearbox. At first, you may well feel something has gone wrong with the linkages—the change is so light and quick that it feels as if something crucial has been disconnected. The fact that everything is still working properly is the reason why most of the other gearboxes made contain some Porsche patents in their design. This one has all of them, and it's a gem. First gear is opposite reverse at the left-hand end of the gate, while second and third, and fourth and fifth are arranged in the normal H formation—this means first and reverse (protected by a strong spring) are together for parking manoeuvres and separate from the open-road gears.

LUGGAGE
There is a long, shallow (11 ins deep) front boot which will hold soft bags and small items of luggage, but the main stowage space is on the baggage platform formed by the folded-down rear seats. The spare wheel is under the floor of the front compartment.

INSTRUMENTS
Five matching dials are set in a row behind the small steering wheel. The left-hand dial is a combined fuel gauge and oil level indicator—this last only shows a reading when the engine is idling and when the oil itself is fully warmed up, thanks to the dry-sump lubrication system. The next dial contains gauges for oil temperature and oil pressure, the largest central dial is a rev-counter, with a red band marked at 7200 rpm, and the two right-hand dials are a speedometer and an electric clock. Separate warning lights monitor alternator, direction signals, headlamp main beam, parking lights and handbrake. A steering column stalk switch controls headlamp dipping and flashing, direction indicators, parking lights — a second stalk switch looks after the three-speed wipers and electric screenwashers.

BRAKING
Brakes are unassisted ventilated discs on all four wheels, with separate drums on rear wheels for handbrake. (front) 10.6 in diameter/discs with 183 sq in swept area. (Rear) 11.0 in diameter discs with 177 sq in swept area. Brakes required firm pedal pressure, but pulled car up effectively with negligible signs of fade (see graph).

Gearbox
Five-speed all-sychromesh unit. Ratios: First—3.09 to 1; second—1.89 to 1; third—1.32 to 1; fourth—1.04 to 1; top 0.79 to 1. Final drive ratio: 4.43 to 1. Type: Spiral bevel.

Suspension
Front—McPherson struts with lower wishbones, longitudinal torsion bars telescopic dampers and anti-roll bar.

Rear—Independent, with semi-trailing arms and transverse torsion bars, telescopic dampers and anti-roll bar.

FUEL CONSUMPTION
Touring open-road consumption 25 mpg.
High-speed—16 mpg.
Town driving—15 mpg.
Overall consumption—18 mpg
Tank capacity—13½ gallons, giving an average range of 240 miles approx.

Porsche 911S
Competition Record

Date	Race	Drivers	Position
6 Feb 1972	Six Hours of Daytona	Peter Gregg/ Hurley Haywood	7th place
6 Feb 1972	Six Hours of Daytona	Jim Locke/ Bob Bailey	10th place
6 Feb 1972	Six Hours of Daytona	Peter Kirill/ Russ Norburn	14th place
25 March 1972	Florida International 12 Hour G.P.	Peter Gregg/ Hurley Haywood	5th place
25 March 1972	Florida International 12 Hour G.P.	Bruce Jennings/ Bob Beasley	11th place
25 March 1972	Florida International 12 Hour G.P.	Erwin Kremer/ Carlos Bolands	12th place
25 March 1972	Florida International 12 Hour G.P.	Peter Kirill/ Russ Norburn	14th place
3 April 1972	7th ADAC 300 km Races	John Fitzpatrick	1st place (2h 24m 26.7s)
3 April 1972	7th ADAC 300 km Races	Claude Haldi	2nd place (2h 24m 57.8s)
3 April 1972	7th ADAC 300 km Races	Günter Steckkönig	3rd place (2h 25m 7.7s)
3 April 1972	7th ADAC 300 km Races	Clemens Schikentanz	4th place (2h 26m 20.1s)
3 April 1972	7th ADAC 300 km Races	Paul Keller	5th place (2h 28m 25.3s)
3 April 1972	7th ADAC 300 km Races	Florian Vetsch	7th place (2h 31m 51.0s)
3 April 1972	7th ADAC 300 km Races	Frank Gerlach	8th place (2h 32m 21.7s)
3 April 1972	7th ADAC 300 km Races	Georg Loos	10th place (2h 32m 21.7s)
16 April 1972	Paris Grand Prix	Claude Ballot-Lena	1st place (1h 22m 9.4s)
16 April 1972	Paris Grand Prix	Paul Keller	3rd place (1h 22m 9.4s)
16 April 1972	Paris Grand Prix	Claude Haldi	4th place (1h 22m 55.0s)
16 April 1972	Paris Grand Prix	Georg Loos	5th place
16 April 1972	Paris Grand Prix	Florian Vetsch	6th place
16 April 1972	Paris Grand Prix	"Bardini"	7th place
16 April 1972	Paris Grand Prix	Sylvain Garant	8th place
16 April 1972	Paris Grand Prix	Eberhard Sindel	10th place
21 May 1972	Targa Florio Group 5 & 4	Pino Pica/ Gabrielle Gottifredi	5th place
21 May 1972	Targa Florio Group 5 & 4	Günter Steckkönig/ Giulio Pucci	6th place

Porsche 911S Competition Record

Date	Race	Drivers	Position
21 May 1972	Targa Florio Group 5 & 4	Jürgen Barth/ Michael Keyser	10th place
21 May 1972	Targa Florio Group 5 & 4	Girolamo Capra/ Angelino Lepri	17th place
21 May 1972	9th Montseny Hillclimb, Spain	Toni Fischhaber	9th place
28 May 1972	ADAC 1000 kms	Erwin Kremer/ John Fitzpatrick	8th place
28 May 1972	ADAC 1000 kms	Günter Steckkönig/ Dieter Schmidt	9th place
28 May 1972	ADAC 1000 kms	Clemens Schickentanz/ Willi Kauhsen	11th place
28 May 1972	ADAC 1000 kms	Jürgen Barth/ Michael Keyser	12th place
28 May 1972	ADAC 1000 kms	Toni Fischhaber/ Leopald Prinz von Bayern	13th place
28 May 1972	ADAC 1000 kms	Claude Haldi/ Bernard Chenevière	20th place
10-11 June 1972	Le Mans 24 Hours	Sylvain Garant/ Jürgen Barth	13th place
18 June 1972	European GT Trophy, Zandvoort	Jürgen Neuhaus	1st place (1h 7m 52.8s)
18 June 1972	European GT Trophy, Zandvoort	John Fitzpatrick	2nd place
18 June 1972	European GT Trophy, Zandvoort	Claude Ballot-Lena	3rd place
18 June 1972	European GT Trophy, Zandvoort	Günter Steckkönig	4th place
18 June 1972	European GT Trophy, Zandvoort	Clemens Schikentanz	5th place
18 June 1972	European GT Trophy, Zandvoort	Roland Larsson	6th place
18 June 1972	European GT Trophy, Zandvoort	Bernard Chenevière	7th place
18 June 1972	European GT Trophy, Zandvoort	Frank Gerlach	9th place
18 June 1972	European GT Trophy, Zandvoort	"Bandini"	10th place
18 June 1972	Mont Ventoux Hillclimb, France	Gérard Larrousse	8th place (10m 53.0s)
18 June 1972	Mont Ventoux Hillclimb, France	Toni Fischhaber	10th place (11m 1.3s)

Porsche 911S Competition Record

Date	Race	Drivers	Position
25 June 1972	Osterreichring 1000 kms	Günter Steckkönig/ Bjorn Waldegaard	10th place
25 June 1972	Osterreichring 1000 kms	Erwin Kremer/ John Fitzpatrick	13th place
2 July 1972	Benelux Cups, Nivelles, Belgium	Bengt Ekberg	3rd place
2 July 1972	Benelux Cups, Nivelles, Belgium	John Fitzpatrick	4th place
2 July 1972	Benelux Cups, Nivelles, Belgium	Jürgen Neuhaus	5th place
2 July 1972	Benelux Cups, Nivelles, Belgium	Günter Steckkönig	6th place
2 July 1972	Benelux Cups, Nivelles, Belgium	Clemens Schickentanz	7th place
2 July 1972	Benelux Cups, Nivelles, Belgium	"Bardini"	8th place
2 July 1972	Trento-Bondone Hillclimb, Italy	Silvano Frisori	1st place (14m 6.25s)
2 July 1972	Trento-Bondone Hillclimb, Italy	Toni Fischhaber	3rd place (14m 21.99s)
2 July 1972	Trento-Bondone Hillclimb, Italy	Pino Pica	5th place (14m 26.62s)
2 July 1972	Trento-Bondone Hillclimb, Italy	Ennio Bonomelli	6th place (14m 37.63s)
2 July 1972	Trento-Bondone Hillclimb, Italy	Sepp Greger	8th place (14m 40.25s)
2 July 1972	Trento-Bondone Hillclimb, Italy	Giovanni Boeris	10th place (14m 47.60s)
22 July 1972	Watkins Glen 6 Hours	Michael Keyser/ Bob Beasley	7th place
22 July 1972	Watkins Glen 6 Hours	David Helmick/ John O'Stean	8th place
30 July 1972	Nurburgring Trophy, West Germany	John Fitzpatrick	1st place (1h 30m 8.4s)
30 July 1972	Nurburgring Trophy, West Germany	Jürgen Neuhaus	2nd place (1h 30m 45.1s)
30 July 1972	Nurburgring Trophy, West Germany	Clemens Schickentanz	3rd place (1h 31m 25.5s)
30 July 1972	Nurburgring Trophy, West Germany	Claude Haldi	4th place (1h 32m 16.6s)
30 July 1972	Nurburgring Trophy, West Germany	Horst Klauke	5th place (1h 35m 11.8s)
30 July 1972	Nurburgring Trophy, West Germany	Ennio Bonomelli	6th place (1h 35m 12.0s)

Porsche 911S
Competition Record

Date	Race	Drivers	Position
30 July 1972	Nurburgring Trophy, West Germany	Kurt Simonsen	7th place (1h 36m 13.4s)
30 July 1972	Nurburgring Trophy, West Germany	"Bardini"	9th place (1h 37m 17.3s)
30 July 1972	Nurburgring Trophy, West Germany	Eugen Kiemele	10th place (1h 38m 24.2s)
27 August 1972	Automobile Club of Switzerland G.P. at Hockenheim, Germany	John Fitzpatrick	1st place (1h 38m 3.1s)
27 August 1972	Automobile Club of Switzerland G.P. at Hockenheim, Germany	Bengt Ekberg	2nd place (1h 39m 21.1s)
27 August 1972	Automobile Club of Switzerland G.P. at Hockenheim, Germany	Claude Haldi	3rd place (1h 39m 50.5s)
27 August 1972	Automobile Club of Switzerland G.P. at Hockenheim, Germany	Erwin Kremer	5th place (1h 40m 40.4s)
27 August 1972	Automobile Club of Switzerland G.P. at Hockenheim, Germany	Thomas Datzmann	6th place (1h 41m 12.8s)
27 August 1972	Automobile Club of Switzerland G.P. at Hockenheim, Germany	Eberhard Sindel	7th place (1h 41m 49.1s)
27 August 1972	Automobile Club of Switzerland G.P. at Hockenheim, Germany	Theo Hofer	8th place
27 August 1972	Automobile Club of Switzerland G.P. at Hockenheim, Germany	Manfred Laub	9th place
10 September 1972	Inter-Europe Cup, Monza	John Fitzpatrick	1st place (1h 12m 43.2s)
10 September 1972	Inter-Europe Cup, Monza	Ennio Bonomelli	2nd place (1h 13m 18.0s)
10 September 1972	Inter-Europe Cup, Monza	Claude Haldi	5th place (1h 14m 42.5s)
10 September 1972	Inter-Europe Cup, Monza	Erwin Kremer	7th place
10 September 1972	Inter-Europe Cup, Monza	Bernard Chenevière	10th place
14-24 September 1972	Tour de France	Jean-Francois Piot/ Guy-Michel Vial	4th place (3h 12m 18.0s)
14-24 September 1972	Tour de France	Raymond Tourol/ Piere Lafont	6th place (3h 17m 4.2s)

Porsche 911S
Competition Record

Date	Race	Drivers	Position
14-24 September 1972	Tour de France	Henri Balas/ Foucher	7th place (3h 17m 24.2s)
14-24 September 1972	Tour de France	Dominique Thiry/ Robert Witz	9th place (3h 23m 14.3s)
12 November 1972	Automobile Club of Portugal G.P.	John Fitzpatrick	1st place (1h 14m 49.91s)
12 November 1972	Automobile Club of Portugal G.P.	Jürgen Neuhaus	2nd place (1h 15m 15.16s)
12 November 1972	Automobile Club of Portugal G.P.	Bengt Ekberg	3rd place (1h 15m 18.56s)
12 November 1972	Automobile Club of Portugal G.P.	Claude Haldi	6th place
12 November 1972	Automobile Club of Portugal G.P.	António Borghes	8th place
3-4 February 1973	12th 24 Hours of Daytona, Florida	George Stone/ Bruce Jennings/ Mike Downs	4th place
3-4 February 1973	12th 24 Hours of Daytona, Florida	John Fitzpatrick/ Erwin Kremer/ Paul Keller	6th place
3-4 February 1973	12th 24 Hours of Daytona, Florida	Tony Adamowicz/ Michael Keyser/ Bob Beasley	8th place
3-4 February 1973	12th 24 Hours of Daytona, Florida	Sepp Greger/ Kurt Hild/ Dieter Schmid	9th place
3-4 February 1973	12th 24 Hours of Daytona, Florida	Bob Bergstrom/ Jim Cook	10th place
3-4 February 1973	12th 24 Hours of Daytona, Florida	David Helmick/ John O'Steen/ Steve Behr	11th place
3-4 February 1973	12th 24 Hours of Daytona, Florida	Klaus Selbert/ Marvin Schoenfeld/ Robert Klempel	14th place
13 May 1973	57th Targa Florio, Italy	Girolamo Capra/ Angelino Lepri	12th place
27 May 1973	ADAC 1000 kms, West Germany	Wagner/ Babendererde	19th place
1 April 1973	ADAC 300 km Races, West Germany	Kurt Simonsen	3rd place (2h 10m 42.8s)
1 April 1973	ADAC 300 km Races, West Germany	Holger Zeller	5th place (2h 13m 0.7s)
1 April 1973	ADAC 300 km Races, West Germany	Hans Hargarten	7th place (2h 17m 53.5s)
1 April 1973	ADAC 300 km Races, West Germany	Horst Sasse	10th place (2h 23m 22.6s)

Porsche 911S
Competition Record

Date	Race	Drivers	Position
15 April 1973	Trans-Am 500, Road Atlanta, Georgia	Bob Bergstrom/ Jim Cook	6th place
5 May 1973	Schaefer Trans-Am 500, Limerock Park, Connecticut	Ludwig Heimrath	9th place
13 May 1973	Paris Grand Prix	Guy Gentils	6th place
13 May 1973	Paris Grand Prix	Jean-Marc Guignard	9th place
31 May- 2 June 1973	Semperit Rally, Austria	Haberi/ Pucher	6th place
28 July 1973	Road America Trans-Am, Wisconsin, USA	Ed Wachs	7th place
28 July 1973	Road America Trans-Am, Wisconsin, USA	Dave Causey/ Don Parrish	10th place
19 August 1973	Edmonton Trans-Am, Alberta, Canada	Ludwig Heimrath	6th place
19 August 1973	Edmonton Trans-Am, Alberta, Canada	Don Parrish	7th place
2 September 1973	Intereurope Cup and 6th E. Mattei Trophy, Monza Autodrome, Italy	"Pooky"/ "Tambauto"	8th place
2 September 1973	Intereurope Cup and 6th E. Mattei Trophy, Monza Autodrome, Italy	Jean-Marc Guignard/ Pillon	9th place
17 June 1974	ADAC 300 km Rennen, European GT Championship)	Gerhard Holup	6th place (2h 39m 44.0s)

PORSCHE 911E

New 2.4-liter engine made this Targa almost a match for last year's 911S

CALIFORNIA PROPOSED a law for 1972 that would have required all new cars sold there to operate on 91-octane fuel. Even though the federal government didn't allow the law, most if not all carmakers, domestic and foreign, conformed their cars to it with reduced compression ratios since there was a 3-month lag between the time California passed the law and Washington announced that California couldn't do it.

Most European carmakers, therefore, use different pistons, heads or head gaskets on their U.S. models. Porsche, however, depends far more heavily on the U.S. market than the others, selling over 50 percent of its small production of cars here; so it makes economic sense for Porsche to let the U.S. "dictate" its engine design for all markets. The result: for 1972 all 6-cyl Porsches, even for their home market, have lower compression ratios just like the rest.

But Porsche seems to triumph over adversity. The clever little German factory was ready with a larger-displacement engine, already proven in competition, and the 2341-cc unit (up from 2195) more than offsets the lower compression ratio's effects. The 911T went from 8.6:1 to 7.5:1 but from 125 to 130 net bhp, the E from 9.1:1 to 8.0:1 and from 155 to 165 bhp; and the S from 9.8:1 to 8.5:1 and from 180 to 190 bhp. So where many other makers took lumps both in performance and fuel economy, Porsche suffers only in fuel economy and gains power and torque in all models.

There are several other changes in the 1972 models. The U.S. T model gets fuel injection to replace its carburetors. To take advantage of the larger engine's broader torque band, Porsche has made a 4-speed gearbox, newly designed and stronger, standard on all models—abandoning the standard 5-speed of the E and S. And the 5-speed that's now optional on all 911s is a new one with a new shift pattern that puts the first four speeds in normal H-pattern, 5th over to the right and forward—a change we suggested some time ago. For the first time the semi-automatic Sportomatic is available on the S. The E gets a normal set of steel springs for its front end in place of the hydraulic leveling devices it had, the S comes with a front spoiler that can be put on the other models, and all three now have black, rather than chrome, trim for all external air inlets-outlets.

Every year Porsche makes enough changes to justify a fresh test, so every year we test one of the three 911 models; perhaps the fact that we enjoy Porsches so much has something to do with the custom too. Having done a T and an S the last two years, this year we chose the E. After the initial shock of its predictably higher price—up over $400 despite elimination of the leveling and 5-speed box—the 1972 E delivered some nice surprises.

For a starter, this year's E turns out to be about as quick as last year's S despite the heaviest test weight we've ever run on a Porsche, beating that car to 60 and 100 mph and being only a half-second later in the standing quarter-mile. It can't match the 2.2 S in top speed but that's largely academic in America anyway, and though not as economical of fuel as a 2.2E it betters last year's S in actual miles per gallon while being able to use cheaper fuel. We did, by the way, use 91-octane no-lead for our tests and the E ran on it without any signs of detonation or run-on; this is more than we can say for some other 1972 cars currently in our stable.

The 2.34-liter engine is somewhat more tractable and less temperamental than the earlier engine. It idles smoothly

ROAD TEST
PORSCHE 911E

SCALE: 10" DIVISIONS

PRICE
List price, east coast........$9078
List price, west coast........$9178
Price as tested, west coast..$10,510
 Price as tested includes 5-speed gearbox ($171), alloy wheels wheels ($360), appearance group ($182), metallic paint ($235), AM/FM radio w/elec antenna ($186), tinted glass ($80), wheel-well moldings ($43), prep ($75)

IMPORTER
Porsche Audi Div, VW of America
600 Sylvan Ave.
Englewood Cliffs, N.J. 07631

ENGINE
Type................sohc flat 6
Bore x stroke, mm.....84.0 x 70.4
 Equivalent in........3.31 x 2.77
Displacement, cc/cu in....2341/143
Compression ratio...........8.0:1
Bhp @ rpm...........165 @ 6200
 Equivalent mph..............132
Torque @ rpm, lb-ft..152 @ 4500
 Equivalent mph...............95
Fuel injection...Bosch mechanical
Fuel required......regular, 91-oct
Emission control....fuel injection, engine mods

DRIVE TRAIN
Transmission......5-speed manual
Gear ratios: 5th (0.759).....3.36:1
 4th (0.962)..............4.26:1
 3rd (1.26)...............5.58:1
 2nd (1.83)...............8.12:1
 1st (3.18)..............14.06:1
Final drive ratio............4.43:1

CHASSIS & BODY
Layout....rear engine/rear drive
Body/frame..............unit steel
Brake type...vented disc; 11.1-in. dia front, 11.4-in. rear
 Swept area, sq in..........500
Wheels........forged alloy, 15 x 6J
Tires....Veith-Pirelli Cinturato 72 185/70-VR15
Steering type......rack & pinion
 Overall ratio............17.8:1
 Turns, lock-to-lock..........3.1
 Turning circle, ft..........32.5
Front suspension: MacPherson struts, lower arms, torsion bars, tube shocks
Rear suspension: semi-trailing arms, torsion bars, tube shocks

ACCOMMODATION
Seating capacity, persons........2
Seat width..............2 x 21.0
Head room.................39.5
Seat back adjustment, degrees..75

INSTRUMENTATION
Instruments: 150-mph speedometer, 8000-rpm tach, 99,999 odo, 999.9 trip odo, oil pressure, oil temp, oil level, fuel level, clock
Warning lights: fuel level, brake-on, high beam, directionals, hazard

MAINTENANCE
Service intervals, mi:
 Oil change..............10,000
 Filter change...........10,000
 Chassis lube.............none
 Tuneup.................10,000
Warranty, mo/mi.......24/24,000

GENERAL
Curb weight, lb..............2485
Test weight.................2845
Weight distribution (with driver), front/rear, %....42/58
Wheelbase, in...............89.5
Track, front/rear........54.1/53.3
Overall length..............163.9
 Width....................63.4
 Height...................52.0
Ground clearance.............5.9
Overhang, front/rear....35.0/39.4
Usable trunk space, cu ft......6.0
Fuel tank capacity, U.S. gal...16.4

CALCULATED DATA
Lb/bhp (test weight).........17.2
Mph/1000 rpm (5th gear)....21.1
Engine revs/mi (60 mph)....2850
Piston travel, ft/mi.........1320
R & T steering index.........1.01
Brake swept area sq in/ton....351

ROAD TEST RESULTS

ACCELERATION
Time to distance, sec:
 0–100 ft.................2.4
 0–250 ft.................4.9
 0–500 ft.................8.2
 0–750 ft................10.7
 0–1000 ft...............13.1
 0–1320 ft (¼ mi).........15.4
Speed at end of ¼ mi, mph..92
Time to speed, sec:
 0–30 mph................2.6
 0–40 mph................3.8
 0–50 mph................5.1
 0–60 mph................6.6
 0–70 mph................9.0
 0–80 mph...............11.5
 0–100 mph..............18.9
Passing exposure time, sec:
 To pass car going 50 mph....5.0

FUEL CONSUMPTION
Normal driving, mpg.........18.6
Cruising range, mi..........305

SPEEDS IN GEARS
5th gear (6450 rpm).........138
4th (7000)..................117
3rd (7000)...................91
2nd (7000)...................63
1st (7000)...................36

HANDLING
Speed on 100-ft radius, mph..33.1
Lateral acceleration, g......0.732

RELIABILITY
From R&T Owner Surveys the average number of trouble areas for all models surveyed is 11. As owners of earlier model Porsche 911 reported 8 trouble areas, we expect the reliability of the 911E to be better than average.

BRAKES
Panic stop from 80 mph:
 Max. deceleration rate, % g..87
 Stopping distance, ft........273
 Control..............very good
Pedal effort for 50%-g stop, lb..40
Fade test: percent increase in pedal effort to maintain 50%-g deceleration rate in 6 stops from 60 mph..................nil
Parking: Hold 30% grade?.....yes
Overall brake rating.....excellent

SPEEDOMETER ERROR
30 mph indicated is actually..26.0
40 mph......................36.0
50 mph......................47.0
60 mph......................58.0
70 mph......................69.0
80 mph......................78.0
100 mph.....................98.0
Odometer, 10.0 mi............9.8

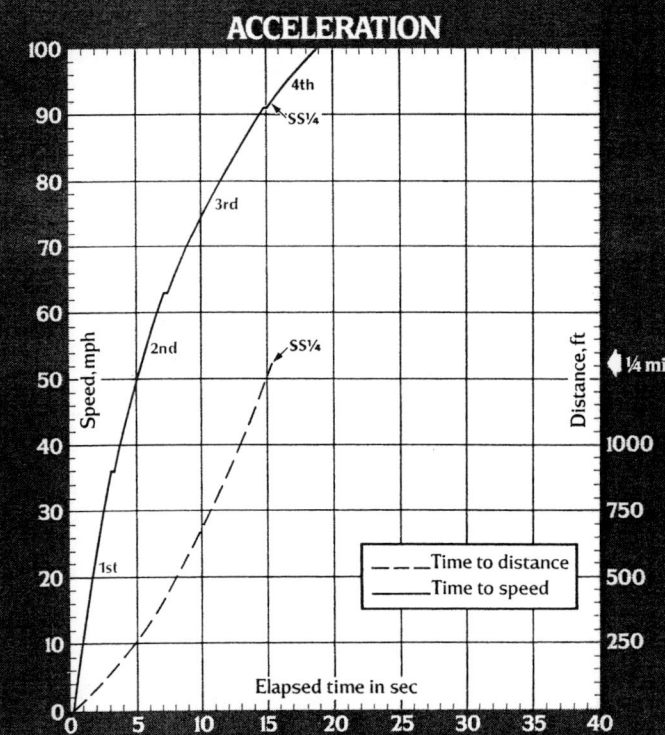

PORSCHE 911E

at 800 rpm and will pull smoothly down to 2000 in any gear but 5th, in which gear rattle gets unpleasant below 2600. There is no need to keep revs up as many Porsche drivers do; the capacitive-discharge ignition keeps the plugs firing even when the engine is deliberately and habitually lugged for hundreds of miles and there is no mechanical damage as long as detonation doesn't occur. Though the latest engine is quieter from inside the car, it is still embarrassingly noisy from outside and this is good reason to keep the revs *down*—consideration for others and all that. Generally the engine runs well without a trace of over-lean mixtures, even when it's cold, but occasionally there's a big backfire on deceleration.

Our test car had the optional 5-speed box, whose new shift pattern is welcome since the first four speeds are the ones most frequently used in everyday driving. Fifth is the "extra" gear and is now located appropriately. The shift linkage, inevitably a bit rubbery because of the distance back to the gearbox, is nevertheless satisfactory and one can make shifts lightning-fast with never a crunch. We wondered, however, why 5th is so noisy, since both it and 4th are overdrives yet 4th is quiet.

Our last two test 911s have had front and rear anti-roll bars, which aren't standard on the E or T. This one didn't and its handling, though still first-class and enjoyable, did not match that of either previous car. The Veith-Pirelli 185/70-15 tires, a bit squishy and squealy at maximum cornering speed, may be partially responsible; in any case this E's 0.732g lateral acceleration falls short of the 0.782g figure we recorded in both those previous road tests with either 185/70 Michelin XVR or 185-14 Michelin XAS tires and anti-roll bars. Braking, however, has benefited from something, perhaps a reapportioning of front-rear effort: we got most impressive stopping distances of 273 ft from 80 mph and 149 ft from 60 mph—the latter only 1 ft off what Porsche's information booklet claims and 6 ft better than the government's Experimental Safety Vehicle requirement. That, friends, is braking.

This was the first Targa we've put through a full test. It's a little heavier than the closed coupe and has more wind noise at speed but otherwise there's little to distinguish it. Body rigidity is still good and it's a matter of personal preference whether or not the lift-off roof is worth the extra $725 it costs. The Targa's esthetics are questionable but that's nothing new; even Ferry Porsche agrees to that.

Any Porsche 911 is very much a driver's car and an experienced and skillful driver can play a 911 as a master violinist plays a Stradivarius. In return for its great potentials of handling, braking and performance one makes certain sporting sacrifices of comfort and quiet, but no true sports car has ever avoided these and the 911E is as good a compromise as any. For those who can do with less than the E's brilliant acceleration there's the T and for those who must have the most there's the S; any one of the three is one of the best sports cars money can buy.

Without anti-roll bars and XVR tires the 911E's cornering performance is reduced to merely "very good."

THE owning and running of Porsches is best described as a contagious ailment, and each succeeding new model seems to make the possibility of becoming an addict the more likely. The latest version has been improved by the use of fuel injection, self-levelling front suspension, a longer wheelbase, and a most ingenious and effective form of semi-automatic transmission. The last three items could, no doubt, be described as concessions to the lazy and average driver, but it must be stressed that cars using the clutchless transmission have already twice won the arduous 84-hour Marathon de la Route. It is of interest that, since the introduction of this model, it has attracted over 50 per cent of all Porsche sales in the UK; the balance being of those models not using the semi-automatic transmission. The 911E can be regarded as the standard version of the six-cylinder Porsche, there being a lower powered "economy" version— the 911T—with 110 b.h.p., and the high-powered 911S with 170 b.h.p. The 911E falls between the two with 140 b.h.p.

All Porsches have gained appreciably from the firm's very active interest in competition work, almost since its earliest days, when it was a derivative of the Volkswagen, and the latest models are no exception. The air-cooled, horizontally opposed, six-cylinder engine uses Bosch fuel injection in place of the more usual carburettors, with a consequent increase in the power output of 10. While a compression ratio of 9·1 to 1 is used the engine will run happily on four-star petrol.

The cooling is forced through ducting by means of a fan. The capacity is obtained by the over-square dimensions of 80 by 66 mm. The total power output of 140 b.h.p. is delivered at 6,500 r.p.m., and the maximum torque at 4,500 r.p.m. If the potential performance is used to the full the car remains within the legal limit on 1st gear alone. The gearing is such that the maxima on the three lower gears are 55, 80 and 107 m.p.h.

Compared with earlier Porsches, the wheelbase of the 911E has been increased by 2·25 in., and at the same time the front suspension has been modified by using MacPherson struts, wishbones and longitudinal torsion bars, while the hydraulic dampers incorporate self-levelling struts. These last mentioned keep the car at a constant height, regardless of load, and also serve to eliminate any tendency to pitching. The rear suspension is also independent, by means of transverse torsion bars, semi-trailing arms and hydraulic dampers. Dunlop-ATE hydraulic disc brakes are used all round. The ZF rack-and-pinion steering requires only 3·1 turns to change from one lock to the other, which gives a turning circle of 33 ft. 9 in. There are no greasing points on the car. The fuel tank has a capacity of 13·7 gall., and at the cost of reduced luggage space, an optional one of 22 gall. can be fitted. This model uses wider wheels with radial-ply tyres, and their greater dimensions, in conjunction with the longer wheelbase, contribute to the improved road-holding.

Sitting in the driving seat there is only one problem I can think of; that is the proximity of the gear lever, when in reverse, and the handbrake lever. However, this would probably only arise if one were showing off to a Ministry of Transport examiner. It is of interest, and importance to some, that

THE PORSCHE 911E SPORTOMATIC. "It is by far the most outstanding grand touring car available today"

alternative steering column lengths and driving seat heights are available from the concessionaires. The pedals are well placed, and a double size brake-pedal is wisely fitted, with ample room for the left foot beside it. The gears must be manually selected, but an electric-vacuum clutch control frees the clutch through the medium of a touch-sensitive gear lever. The automatic clutch control is so sensitive that the moment the gear lever is touched the lever can be put into the selected position. As this is matched with a torque converter, it is possible to do all one's driving on any selected gear, depending on the mood of the moment. In town driving, for example, the lever can be left in the top gear position. The rear compartment is best regarded as an additional luggage space, although it could in emergency carry two small children. As one expects on any Porsche, the front seats and the layout of the controls set an example to all other manufacturers.

All one's anticipations about the car, based on examination of the specification and faith in the Porsche approach, are confirmed in the first few miles at the wheel, and this is true even if they are in London, or its sprawling suburbs. Earlier Porsches, without the benefits of the Sportomatic transmission, tended to be cars that only came fully to life on the open road. As there is now no need to preoccupy oneself with gear-changing in town, this is one fast GT car that can be driven in traffic in the style of the most thrustful of drivers. There are, no doubt, misguided purists who dislike the use of this type of transmission on such a car as the 911E, but in my opinion this is nonsense. For such drivers there is the 911S with 170 b.h.p. and the wonderful five-speed Porsche gearbox; all models can be had with that form of transmission.

Settling into the car, starting the engine— there are a few seconds lapse while the fuel injection system's brain works out the temperature—and just moving from rest give as much pleasure as the average car could hope to give in its entire life. With the maxima I have mentioned on the lower gears, and an outright maximum of just over 130 m.p.h., allied with a hard driving fuel consumption of just on 20 m.p.g., the car's overall performance tends to be taken for granted, even by relatively timid passengers. What is important is that everything the car can do is carried out impeccably. Either long fast curves, or the sharpest of tightening corners, can be taken with the greatest of ease and security, and relatively inexperienced drivers will find that driving a Porsche, either borrowed, or bought, will improve their driving to a surprising extent.

The Porsche is not as silent as a water-cooled engine, through the lack of the insulating effect of the water jacket. While greater silence would allow an even closer approach to perfection, there are few Porsche owners who would even notice this point, because of their bemused affection for the car's overall characteristics. A rear-mounted air-cooled engine allows the heating system to be a little more leisurely in its effect, first thing on a cold morning but, in any case, this impels one to devote a few moments to warming up the car before moving off. These two minor points apart, this latest version of the Porsche enhances the make's already very high reputation. The benefits of fuel injection, self-levelling suspension, longer wheelbase, bigger tyres, and the outstanding overall performance, as well as the exceptional comfort and security of the seating, make the 911E Sportomatic—excluding models intended only for racing—by far the most outstanding grand touring car available to-day.

PORSCHE 911E SPORTOMATIC

Concessionaires: Porsche Cars (Great Britain), London Road, Isleworth, Middlesex.

SPECIFICATION

Price	£4,242	Brakes	Dunlop-ATE disc all round
(including P.T.)	£994		
Cubic capacity	1,991 c.c.	Suspension	Independent all round
Bore and stroke	80 × 66 mm.	Wheelbase	7 ft. 5·5 in.
Cylinders	Six, horizontally opposed	Track (front)	4 ft. 4·5 in.
		Track (rear)	4 ft. 3·7 in.
Valves	Overhead camshaft	Overall length	13 ft. 8 in.
B.h.p. 140 at 6,500 r.p.m.		Overall width	5 ft. 3·5 in.
Carburettor	Bosch fuel injection	Overall height	4 ft. 4 in.
		Ground clearance	6 in.
Ignition	Coil	Turning circle	33 ft. 9 in.
Oil filter	Purolator full-flow	Weight	20·9 cwt.
1st gear	10·63 to 1	Fuel capacity	13·7 galls.
2nd gear	7·22 to 1	Oil capacity	16 pints
3rd gear	5·39 to 1	Water capacity	Nil: air-cooled
4th gear	4·15 to 1	Tyres	Dunlop SP 185 × 15
Final drive	Spiral bevel		

PERFORMANCE

Acceleration		
	Top	3rd
30-50	6·5 secs.	5·5 secs.
40-60	8·0 secs.	6·6 secs.
0-70 (all gears)	12·2 secs.	
Max. speed	133 m.p.h. (estimated)	

Petrol consumption 20 m.p.g. at average speed of 55 m.p.h.

Brakes 30 to 0 in 31 ft (97 per cent efficiency)

Porsche Types 911T – 911E – 911S

ENGINE (Rear)

Type	4-stroke; horizontally-opposed cylinders; single overhead camshaft for each bank
Cooling system	Air; (T) 1230 litres/sec. at 5,800 r.p.m.; (E) (S) 1380 at 6,500
Number of cylinders	6 (dry liners)
Firing order and idling speed	1—6—2—4—3—5 (No. 1 at rear, left); 850/950 r.p.m.
Bore	84mm.
Stroke	66mm.
Cubic capacity	2195c.c.
Compression ratio	(T) 8·6:1; (E) 9·1:1; (S) 9·8:1
Brake horse-power (DIN)	(T) 123 (125PS) at 5,800 r.p.m.; (E) 153 (155PS) at 6,500; (S) 177 (180PS) at 6,500
Torque—kg.m. (lb.ft.)	(T) 18 (130) at 4,200; (E) 19·5 (141) at 4,500; (S) 20·3 (147) at 5,200
Piston clearance in bore	At 30mm below top. (T) Mahle, 0·025/0·045mm.; Schmidt, 0·033/0·058. (E) 0·035/0·055. (S) 0·045/0·065
Piston rings—number	2 compression, 1 oil
Piston rings—width	Comp., 1·5 and 2mm.; oil, 4mm.
Piston rings—groove cl'nce	Comp.: top, 0·075/0·107mm.; lower, 0·060/0·072. Oil, 0·025/0·052
Piston rings—gap (in bore)	All, 0·3 to 0·45mm.
Oil pressure	71/81lb./sq.in. at 80°C. and 5,000r.p.m.
Gudgeon pin diameter	22mm. —0·003 —0·006. Oversize, 22 —0 —0·003
Gudgeon pin fit in piston	Bore diam., 22mm. —0 —0·003
Gudgeon pin fit in con. rod	Bore diam., 22mm. +0·02 +0·039
Crankpin diameter	56·971 to 56·990mm.
Crankpin undersizes	Three
Connecting rod length	130mm. (centres)
Big-end bearings	Tri-metal shells
Big-end bearing clearance	0·03 to 0·088mm.
Big-end side clearance	0·2 to 0·4mm.
Main journal diameter	56·971 to 56·990mm.
Main journal undersizes	Three
Main bearings	7 tri-metal shells plus 1 aluminium
Main bearings—length	7×18mm.; 1×28mm.
Main bearing clearance	0·030 to 0·088mm.
Crankshaft end-float	0·110 to 0·195mm.
Crankshaft end-thrust on	No. 1 bearing (flywheel end)
Camshaft journal diameter	46·926 to 46·942mm.
Camshaft bearings	3 per camshaft
Camshaft bearing cl'nce	0·025 to 0·066mm.
Camshaft end-float	0·150 to 0·200mm.
Camshaft drive type	Duplex chain
Valve head diameter	Inlet, 46mm.; exhaust, 40mm.
Valve stem diameter	Inlet, 8·97 —0·012mm.; exhaust, 8·95 —0·012mm.
Valve seat angle	45° (face angles, 75°/30°)
Valve lift —Inlet	(T) 9·7mm.; (E) 10·5; (S) 11·6
—Exh.	(T) 8·9mm.; (E) 9·7; (S) 10·3
Valve guide length	51·2 —0·4mm.; fitted height, 13·2 —0·3mm. above head
Valve stem/guide cl'nce	Inlet, 0·03/0·057mm.; exh., 0·05/0·077mm.
Valve spring free length	Inner, 38·4mm.; outer, 41·8mm.
Valve spring rate	Inner, 22·7mm. at 34·5kg. (76lb.); outer, 35mm. at 17kg. (37·5lb.)
Valve working clearance	0·1mm. (·0039in.) cold, inlet and exh.
Valve timing clearance	1mm. (·039in.)

Valve timing—

	T	E	S
Inlet opens	15° B.T.	20° B.T.	38° B.T.
Inlet closes	29° A.B.	34° A.B.	50° A.B.
Exhaust opens	41° B.B.	40° B.B.	40° B.B.
Exhaust closes	5° B.T.	6° A.T.	20° A.T.

Porsche Types 911T – 911E – 911S

FUEL SYSTEM
Petrol pump ... Bosch, electric
Carburettors ... 2 Solex-Zenith 40TIN | Bosch fuel injection
Choke tube ... 27·5
Main jet ... 115
Compensating jet ... 185
Slow-running jet ... 47·5
Slow-running air bleed ... 1·4
Emulsion tube ... K25 069
Needle valve ... 1·5mm.

Inj. pressure: 15/18 atmos. (220/265 lb./sq.in.)
Inj. timing: inj. ends 40° A.T.D.C.

TRANSMISSION
Type ... Rear engine (behind axle)
Clutch ... Fichtel & Sachs, 225mm. (8·9in.)
Gearbox (manual) ... (T) 4- or 5-speed, (E) (S) 5-speed all synchro.
Gearbox (automatic) ... 'Sportomatic' optional for (T) & (E)
Gearbox ratios—4-speed 0·759; 1·040; 1·632; 3·091; R., 3·13:1
—5-speed 0·759; 0·926; 1·218; 1·778; 3·091; R., 3·13:1
Driving axles ... Double-jointed half-shafts
Final drive gear ... Spiral bevel
Final drive ratio ... 4·429:1 (31/7)
Crown wheel/pinion b'lash 0·12/0·18mm. (·005/·007in.)
Diff. bearing pre-load ... SKF, 0·25/0·35kg.m. (21·7/30·3lb.in.)
FAG, 0·40/0·65kg.m. (34·7/56·4lb.in.)

BRAKES (Dual-circuit)
Front ... ATE/Porsche, 235mm. (9·25in.) discs
Rear ... ATE/Porsche, 244mm. (9·6in.) discs
Handbrake ... Mechanical, on separate rear drums
Linings—front ... Area per wheel 76cm.^{2} (11·8sq.in.)
Linings—rear ... Area per wheel 52·5cm.^{2} (8·1sq.in.)

STEERING (see also "Dimensions")
Type ... ZF, rack and pinion
Camber angle ... 0°±20'
Castor angle ... 6° 45'±45'
King-pin inclination ... 10° 56'
Toe-in/Toe-out ... 0°, under 15kg. (35lb.) pressure
Conditions for checking... Unladen (tank full)

FRONT SUSPENSION
Type ... Longitudinal torsion bars; shock-absorber struts or self-levelling hydropneumatic struts (standard for 'E')

REAR SUSPENSION
Type ... Transverse torsion bars and semi-trailing arms
Wheel camber ... —50'±20'
Toe-in/Toe-out ... 0°+10' each wheel

Porsche Types 911T – 911E – 911S

ELECTRICAL SYSTEM

Ignition timing—static	T.D.C. (mark on pulley)
—stroboscope	At 6,000 r.p.m.: (T) 35°, (E) (S) 30° B.T.D.C.
Sparking plugs	(T) Beru 240/14/3 (in U.S.A. 250/14/3P) or Bosch W230T3 (U.S.A., W250P21); (E) (S) Bosch W265P21 or Beru [265/14/3P
Sparking plug gap	All 0·6mm. (·0236in.)
Distributor	(T) Marelli S112BX; (E) Bosch JFDR6 0231159006; (S) JFDR6 0231159007
Contact breaker gap	0·4mm. (·0157in.); dwell angle 38°±3°
Centrif. advance starts at	Max. 3° A.T.D.C. at 1,000 r.p.m. (crank.)
Centrif. advance—max.	Max. 35° B.T.D.C. at 6,000 r.p.m. (crank.)
Ignition coil	Bosch 0 221 121 001
Battery	2×12v. 36a.h.
Battery earth	Negative
Alternator	Bosch, 770 watts
Starter motor	Bosch EB(L) 12v 0·8PS (horse-power)

CAPACITIES

Engine sump	(T) (E) 9 litres (15·8 pints); auto., 11 litres (19·4p.). (S) 10 litres (17·6 pints)
Gearbox	} 2·5 litres (4·4 pints)
Differential	
Fuel tank	62 litres (13·6 galls.) incl. 6 l. (1·3g.) reserve
Tyre size	(E) (S) and optional (T) 185/70VR15; (T) std., 165 HR15 (auto., 185HR14)
Tyre pressures —Front	1·8 atmos. (26lb./sq.in.)
—Rear	2·0 atmos. (29lb./sq.in.)
No. of grease gun points	Nil
Servicing intervals	Engine oil change (inc. filter) 6,000 miles
Hydraulic fluid	ATE

DIMENSIONS

Length overall	4163mm. (13ft. 7·9in.)
Width overall	1610mm. (63·4in.)
Height overall	1320mm. (52·0in.)
Weight (kerb)	1020kg. (2249lb. or 20·1cwt.)
Ground clearance (laden)	150mm. (5·9in.)
Track—(T)	F., 1362mm. (53·6in); R., 1343mm. (52·9in.)
—(E) & (S)	F., 1374mm. (54·1in.); R., 1355mm. (53·3in.)
Wheelbase	2268mm. (89·3in.)
Turning circle diameter	10·7m. (35·1ft.)

TORQUE SPANNER DATA

	kg.m.	lb.ft.
Cylinder head nuts	3·0/3·3	21·7/23·8
Big-end bearing nuts	5	36·2
Flywheel bolts	15	108
Clutch to flywheel bolts	2·1/2·3	15·2/16·6
Final drive pinion bearing nut	11/12	79·6/86·8
Crown wheel bolts	9·5/10	68·7/72·3
Road wheel nuts	12	86·8
Steering wheel nut	8	57·8

BODY AND CHASSIS

Type of construction …
Material of body panels…
Windscreen glass …

CAR and DRIVER ROAD TEST

Porsche 911 Sportomatic

Like the car itself, Porsche's "automatic" transmission takes a bit of getting used to

You really don't suppose that the *Herren Doktoren* at Porsche really believe all that FIA stuff about the 911 being a Group II *sedan*?

On the other hand, how do you explain Stuttgart's new Sportomatic transmission? If the 911 was a legitimate 4-passenger sedan, instead of a precise, responsive *Gran Turismo*, the Sportomatic might be a nifty option. But despite what the FIA has said, the 911 is a GT, and we can't reconcile ourselves to the fact that Porsche would sacrifice so much to develop a new market. Say it isn't so.

It is. Sportomatic, which is nothing more than the time-honored Porsche 4-speed transmission connected to the engine with an automatic clutch and a torque converter, is now available on all 911s. And we don't like it. We understand the reasons for it, but we disagree and we don't like it.

Follow the reasoning of Porsche's product planners. The traffic situation in metropolitan areas gets worse by the day and there's no relief in sight. People are here to stay, and people drive cars, and more and more of them, and those cars clog the highways. Even die-hard sports car buffs have been known to grow weak after continued exposure to rush-hour traffic if only in half-hour, morning and evening increments. There is the purist stuck on the Bayshore Freeway or the East Side Drive and it takes him an hour to drive five miles—bumper to bumper—and his left leg begins to tie up and he's got a charley horse that would put a pentathlon star to shame and he begins to wonder if there isn't something better.

Porsche did some wondering too, and Porsche's answer was the Sportomatic. Trouble is, Porsche should have held out. Porsche is *the* enthusiast's car. It's not cheap, but it's not up there with Lamborghini either. It's comfortable, it handles, and it goes—even as a Group 2 sedan, maybe especially as a Group 2 sedan. It would be easier to discover your wife was unfaithful than Porsche—but that's not the way Porsche thought of it.

Porsche thought it had a perfect car for the enthusiast and non-enthusiast alike. Maybe the car's bumper protection really isn't up to the task of defending the 911 against onslaughts from arrogant buses and taxis, but with Porsche's agility and modest size that kind of defense shouldn't really be necessary. Just give us an automatic transmission—Porsche thought—and we'll have an everyman's car, everyman who can afford over $6300 that is.

Well, it doesn't work. Not only is Sportomatic a funny name, but the transmission is a funny transmission—though there is little humor in the added $280 tacked on because they've taken away the clutch. The whole thing puts you to mind of Detroit's bizarre efforts at clutchless shifting that died a merciful death in the middle Fifties. The great unlamented Gyromatic, for instance. If the Gyromatic didn't put Chrysler Corporation out of business, it hurt—and hurt badly; and we're sad to see Porsche repeat the experiment.

Porsche begins by calling its Sportomatic an automatic transmission, and you'd think, if you didn't know any better, that the transmission would change gears by itself. No chance. And in this day of computers and automation, being required to *shift* an automatic is a hard fault to overlook. It's unlikely Porsche is trying to deceive anyone except themselves, but the fact remains that they've labeled the gear shift knob L-D-D3 and D4 in the Sportomatic. Save your stamps if you're interested in finding where D2 went. We haven't a clue. A thorough search uncovered not a single trace of it, and we looked hard. Its whereabouts will forever remain one of the mysteries of the Sportomatic.

But P is a good lick. Everyone should have a parking lock, even if it's only so you can concentrate at the drive-in.

So Porsche wanted to sell more cars—wanted to have a broader market base—and decided the time-honored automatic clutch was the answer. As we said, it's nothing new. There's a whole untapped market out there made up of people whose level of coordination won't allow them to put any kind of sequence at all to the movements of a clutch pedal and gear shift lever. And it's obvious Porsche had them very much in

43

Brace yourself, world: there's a whole new breed of Porsche-lovers on tap thanks to the Sportomatic

mind. Even near imperceptible movements of the shift lever actuates a microswitch which, through a solenoid, activates a vacuum system. A single plate dry clutch, inspired by a vacuum cylinder, interrupts torque flow so the manual transmission can be shifted. The purpose of the torque converter is clear: it allows the 911 to be stopped with the brake without declutching or engaging neutral. Moreover, it multiplies engine torque in the lower speed ranges to reduce the need for selecting a lower gear when greater acceleration is required.

All of which is to say that *driving* a Sportomatic is not difficult, but enjoying it would require concentrated effort and no previous exposure to the delights of the manual car—a lovely, exciting, *satisfying* device.

In explaining how all this works, Porsche encourages you to engage D when and if you choose to move forward. Use L when ascending or descending steep grades. Cope with ice and ennui as best you can—a problem that Porsche has never had before.

D was dutifully selected and a moderate depression of the throttle opened all six Weber throttles in absolutely normal fashion. The result was a healthy roar from the engine compartment with a sadly disproportionate amount of forward progress. Any major throttle opening with the transmission in any of the D positions causes the tach to zoom up to about 3000 rpm and hang there until the car catches up. As a matter of fact, one of our biggest objections to the Sportomatic was trying to distinguish any one D from any other D. They all seemed the same. The engine sounded the same, the performance seemed about equal and we just didn't know what to make of it.

Happily, once you get the thing over 3000 rpm, the system acts much more like a manual transmission. A little experimenting with the not-recommended L position resulted in an engine roar much more in keeping with the car's speed and, better still, it reduced quarter-mile times by a half a second. Not bad. Don't be alarmed, Porsche lovers, L is simply first gear in the manual transmission, so there is no reason why it shouldn't be used for acceleration as well as braking.

One more moment of carping: you will remember we said that the clutch is automatically disengaged with even imperceptible movements of the shift lever. We weren't kidding. The driver had better remember precisely where the shift lever is, because if he so much as *rests* his hand on it before he is ready to shift, the clutch will disengage and the tach will whirl out of sight before you can say "holy broken motor." Porsche claims to have an automatic ignition cut-out, but who wants to see if it works?

With all this, it's about time to make it clear that there's absolutely no trouble in shifting. Just grab the lever and move it. No matter how fast you do it, it's *impossible* to beat the clutch or the synchronizers. And that's a real pay raise if you want a Porsche and your wife doesn't because she doesn't think she'll be able to drive it. She will, and easily, too. And maybe that's one of our objections. You may find yourself a little embarrassed when you're trying to make a quick shift because the sound put out for the world to hear is a pretty strong implication that the driver doesn't know when it's safe to let the clutch out.

So you're driving the Sportomatic with your hand poised, hawk-like, in mid-air, awaiting the proper time to swoop down on the lever. But it might be well to remember that the hawk-like hand isn't the only thing ever to hit that lever. You can do it with your knee under hard cornering—and who wants a Porsche if he isn't going to bend it in a corner now and then—and if you go for the fast idle or heater controls located between the seats, and miss, you might find yourself in D3.

So we're unhappy. And we're unhappy because the 911 is still something of a standard for judging roadholding and ultimate cornering ability. We were pleasantly surprised to learn that those unfashionable 4.5-inch wide wheels used on Porsches almost since day one have been replaced by wheels an inch wider. Racing seems to have improved the breed here, and Porsche, which stormed off with the under 2-liter championship in the '67 Trans-Am series,

has obviously paid attention to how they accomplished that. Ride harshness suffers, but what the hell, it's a Porsche, and Porsches are *cars*.

Porsche handling has usually generated debate among the oversteer-understeer factions. We like it, it's got style and it works. Hang the tail out, put a wheel in the air and grab a handful of reverse lock, we say. On the other hand, we do recommend that a newcomer to the car approach it with great respect. The transition from initial understeer to mild oversteer can be disconcerting to the novice.

Another thing the 911 does well is stop. The truly sophisticated internally vented disc brakes on all four wheels pull the car down at a .91G deceleration rate in our 80 to 0 mph braking test. More than that, not a trace of fade was apparent after four stops. This kind of performance is vastly superior to what we've grown to expect from the more conventional disc front/drum rear systems on so many American and European cars.

Several visible changes have been made in the car for '68 so that they will comply with the federal government's safety and exhaust emission standards. The windshield wiper arms are now flat black and, for some reason, come to rest in front of the driver instead of on the passenger side as on earlier 911s. Porsche styling has generally been way ahead of the pack, particularly in the lighting department. The car's parking and tail lights are of wrap-around design which makes them visible from the sides as well as the front and rear. Even so, Porsche has added reflectors on the sides of both front and rear fenders—and the result is that a Porsche will never go unnoticed at night. Besides, what better way to tell a '68 from a pre-federal safety standard 911?

Another, sadder, change is the absence of the 911S. The 180 hp car is no longer available in this country thanks to the benevolent legislators and the smog laws. Porsche engineers weren't able to strain enough carbon monoxide and unburned hydrocarbons out of the exhaust and still have 180 horsepower left for the customer, so they've concentrated their efforts on the 148 hp version. Porsche has used the typically European approach to the exhaust emission control problem, choosing the afterburning process in which fresh air is pumped into the exhaust manifold resulting in rapid oxidation of large clouds of evil gasses. Installation of all the required plumbing has made the engine compartment crowded, but aside from the clutter no undesirable effects resulted. Besides, what-

PORSCHE 911 SPORTOMATIC

Importer: Porsche of America Corp.
107 Tryon Ave. West
Teaneck, N.J.

Number of dealers in U.S.: 244

Vehicle type: Rear-engine, rear-wheel-drive, 2+2-passenger GT coupe

Price as tested: $7156.00
(Manufacturer's suggested retail price, including all options listed below, Federal excise tax, dealer preparation and delivery charges; does not include state and local taxes, license or freight charges)

Options on test car: Sportomatic ($280), tinted glass ($75), bumper guards ($16), auxiliary heater ($220), Dunlop tires ($45), chrome wheels ($100), AM/FM/SW radio ($240), wood-rim steering wheel $($60), special paint ($130)

ENGINE
Type: Air-cooled flat six, aluminum block and heads, 8 main bearings
Bore x stroke...3.15 x 2.60 in, 80.0 x 66.0 mm
Displacement...............121.5 cu in, 1991cc
Compression ratio.......................9.0 to one
Carburetion........2 x 3-bbl Weber 46 IDA 3C
Valve gear......Single chain-driven overhead camshaft on each bank, rocker arms
Power (SAE)................148 bhp @ 6100 rpm
Torque (SAE).........145 lbs/ft @ 4200 rpm
Specific power output........1.22 bhp/cu in, 74.3 bhp/liter
Max. recommended engine speed...6800 rpm

DRIVE TRAIN
Transmission.........4-speed all-synchro with automatic clutch and torque converter
Clutch diameter....................................7.13 in
Max. torque converter ratio.......2.15 to one
Final drive ratio....................3.86 to one

Gear	Ratio	Mph/1000 rpm	Max. test speed
I	2.40	7.9	54 mph (6800 rpm)
II	1.63	11.6	79 mph (6800 rpm)
III	1.22	15.6	106 mph (6800 rpm)
IV	0.96	19.7	114 mph (5800 rpm)

DIMENSIONS AND CAPACITIES
Wheelbase..................................87.1 in
Track...............F: 53.8 in, R: 52.6 in
Length....................................163.9 in
Width......................................63.4 in
Height.....................................52.0 in
Ground clearance....................5.9 in
Curb weight............................2430 lbs
Test weight.............................2590 lbs
Weight distribution, F/R.....40.6/59.4%
Lbs/bhp (test weight)..................17.5
Battery capacity..........12 volts, 45 amp/hr
Alternator capacity...................420 watts
Fuel capacity...........................16.4 gal
Oil capacity............................12.0 qts

SUSPENSION
F: Ind., MacPherson strut with lower wishbone, longitudinal torsion bars
R: Ind., semi-trailing arms, transverse torsion bars

STEERING
Type.....................Rack and pinion
Turns lock-to-lock...............................2.75
Turning circle.....................................33 ft

BRAKES
F: ATE-Dunlop 11.1-in vented disc
R: ATE-Dunlop 11.25-in vented disc with integral 7.09-in drums for hand brake
Swept area.............................371 sq in

WHEELS AND TIRES
Wheel size and type............15 x 5.5-in, stamped steel, 5-bolt
Tire make, size and type......Dunlop 165 HR 15 SP, radial ply, tube-type
Test inflation pressures...F: 29 psi, R: 32 psi
Tire load rating......810 lbs per tire @ 24 psi

PERFORMANCE
Zero to	Seconds
30 mph	2.7
40 mph	4.4
50 mph	6.4
60 mph	9.3
70 mph	12.2
80 mph	16.0
90 mph	20.2
100 mph	25.7

Standing ¼-mile................16.8 sec @ 82 mph
80–0 mph panic stop................236 ft (.91 G)
Fuel mileage......15–19 mpg on premium fuel
Cruising range......................240–300 mi

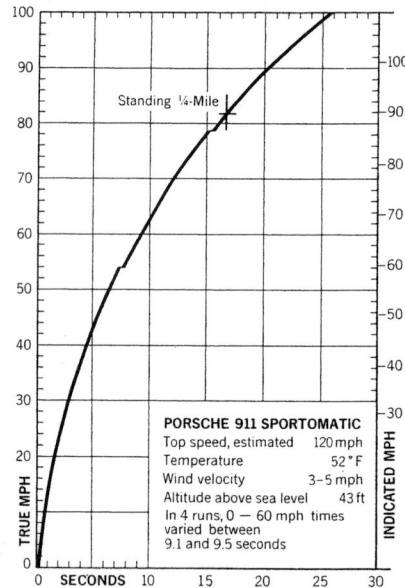

PORSCHE 911 SPORTOMATIC
Top speed, estimated 120 mph
Temperature 52°F
Wind velocity 3–5 mph
Altitude above sea level 43 ft
In 4 runs, 0 — 60 mph times varied between 9.1 and 9.5 seconds

CHECK LIST

ENGINE
Starting..................................Fair
Response...........................Excellent
Vibration...........................Excellent
Noise....................................Fair

DRIVE TRAIN
Shift linkage....................Very Good
Synchro action................Excellent
Clutch smoothness..........Excellent
Drive train noise..............Excellent

STEERING
Effort...................................Good
Response...........................Excellent
Road feel..........................Excellent
Kickback..........................Very Good

SUSPENSION
Ride comfort.......................Good
Roll resistance................Very Good
Pitch control...................Very Good
Harshness control................Good

HANDLING
Directional control...............Good
Predictability......................Fair
Evasive maneuverability...Very Good
Resistance to sidewinds........Fair

BRAKES
Pedal pressure................Very Good
Response..........................Excellent
Fade resistance...............Excellent
Directional stability..............Good

CONTROLS
Wheel position................Excellent
Pedal position................Very Good
Gearshift position................Good
Relationship....................Excellent
Small controls......................Good

INTERIOR
Ease of entry/exit................Good
Noise level (cruising)............Fair
Front seating comfort......Excellent
Front leg room................Excellent
Front head room............Very Good
Front hip/shoulder room.......Good
Rear seating comfort............Poor
Rear leg room.....................Poor
Rear head room..................Poor
Rear hip/shoulder room.......Poor
Instrument comprehensiveness....Excellent
Instrument legibility............Good

VISION
Forward..........................Excellent
Front quarter................Very Good
Side................................Excellent
Rear quarter.......................Fair
Rear....................................Fair

WEATHER PROTECTION
Heater/defroster...............Excellent
Ventilation..........................Fair
Weather sealing.............Very Good

CONSTRUCTION QUALITY
Sheet metal....................Excellent
Paint..............................Excellent
Chrome.........................Very Good
Upholstery.....................Excellent
Padding.........................Very Good
Hardware......................Very Good

GENERAL
Headlight illumination...........Good
Parking and signal lights...Excellent
Wiper effectiveness........Very Good
Service accessibility.............Fair
Trunk space........................Fair
Interior storage space..........Good
Bumper protection...............Fair

46

PORSCHE 911 SPORTOMATIC

ever the virtues of previous Porsches, service accessibility was never among them and, like dueling scars, burns and skinned knuckles have always been a badge of merit among true Porsche lovers.

For any GT car in the $6000 range to be worth its salt, consideration must be given to the driver. After all, these are supposed to be drivers' cars and not family barges. In this area the Porsche really shines. A few hours behind the wheel gives the impression that a driver could set off for the end of the world and still be fresh enough for a return trip without ever getting out. The luxurious bucket seats support just the right portions of the anatomy while the woodrim steering wheel is the proper arms-reach away. Unfortunately, the rim of the wheel obscures the driver's view of the oil level on the left and the clock on the right. This is the only serious flaw in an otherwise well layed-out interior. Since there is no clutch pedal with the Sportomatic, the designers have thoughtfully provided a platform for the driver to rest his left foot. Other manufacturers please copy.

Air-cooled cars are not famous for having the most powerful heaters in the world so auxiliary heaters of some sort are frequently provided. Our test car was equipped with such a device of extraordinary capacity. We fully expect that the interior of this car could be maintained at a comfortably warm temperature in an Alaskan winter even with the doors open.

How, then, does the Sportomatic Porsche fit into the luxury GT car market? Mechanically, we question the wisdom of circulating engine oil and torque converter oil from the same sump even though we know Porsche engineers don't make many mistakes. A definite problem area exists when the clutch can be disengaged by accidental contact with the shift lever even though this is an essential part of the whole automatic clutch system. Still, we grudgingly admit that Porsche has probably increased their market appeal. Any territory gained would be in the non-enthusiast area since we can't conceive of any current Porsche buyers denying themselves the joy of using its faultless 4- or optional 5-speed gearbox or just giving up part of the precision feel of the pre-Sportomatic 911. Non-enthusiasts who could appreciate the Porsche as a fine touring car but have no desire for total involvement in driving technique will be potential customers for the Sportomatic. Somehow, it just seems that Porsche has compromised themselves and this is hard to swallow. Like finding out that your mother is taking in laundry just to put you through school.

We've tested 911s before and come away glowing with admiration. We are still glowing. Unless there are some changes made in the Sportomatic, however, the 911s we will choose in the future will have foot-operated clutches and no torque converters, thank you.

●

"WINDWARD ENTERPRISES INTRODUCES FOR THE FIRST TIME IN THE UNITED STATES!!"

THE FIRST COMPLETE, CONCISE, COMPREHENSIVE REPORT AND SURVEY OF ALL THE GENERALLY RECOGNIZED FORMS OF MOTOR RACING IN THE WORLD

RACEREPORT

coverage	
Group 2	European Touring Car Championship
Group 2	Trans-Am Series
Group 3, 4 & 6	World Manufacturers Trophy
Group 5b	NASCAR Grand National Series
Group 7	CAN-AM Series
Group 8	F3 European Challenge Cup
Group 8	F2 European Challenge Trophy
Group 8	F1 World Championship
Group 9	Formula "V"
Group 9	Indianapolis USAC Championship

COMPLETE WITH OVER 500 INFORMATIVE AND EXCITING ILLUSTRATIONS BY THE WORLD'S BEST AUTO RACING PHOTOGRAPHERS

RACEREPORT IS THE only complete report of ALL the major races in the world in 1967. Featuring over 500 photographs depicting what happened in the world of racing. RACEREPORT is entirely different from what has ever been done before—and most important—it's clearly done—easy to follow and to understand.

RESERVE YOUR COPY NOW . . . RACEREPORT WILL ARRIVE THE FIRST WEEK OF MARCH. RACEREPORT IS ONLY $9.95—ORDER NOW AND SEND ONLY $7.50. MARCH 1, 1968 ALL COPIES WILL BE $9.95.

RACE REPORT

THE MOST COMPLETE COLLECTION OF 1967 WORLD RACING STATISTICS COMPILED AND AVAILABLE TODAY.

exclusive north american distributor
windward enterprises
po box 511
narberth, penn. 19072

Mail to: WINDWARD ENTERPRISES
P. O. Box 511, Narberth, Penn. 19072
Please reserve _____ copy(s) RACEREPORT.
SAVE — ORDER NOW — SAVE
Enclose check or money order now and pay only $7.50 ea. After March 1, 1968—$9.95.
SEND TO:
NAME_____
ADDRESS_____
STATE_____ ZIP_____

See the world's greatest cars at the world's most exciting auto show!

International Automobile Show
March 30 – April 7

It's here...the auto *Event* of the year! Over 500 fabulous cars from England, France, Germany, Italy, Japan, Sweden, the U.S.A....many making their *world premieres*. Devil-may-care motorcycles, sporty scooters and exciting accessories, too. Colorful movies...plus the great cars of yesterday, today, and tomorrow. See the much-heralded electric car of the future! It's the greatest Auto Show since the invention of the wheel! So...GO-GO-GO!

new york coliseum

Adults: $2.50   Children (under 12) $1.00 • Mon. thru Sat. 11 a.m.-11 p.m. Sun. 1 p.m.-8 p.m.

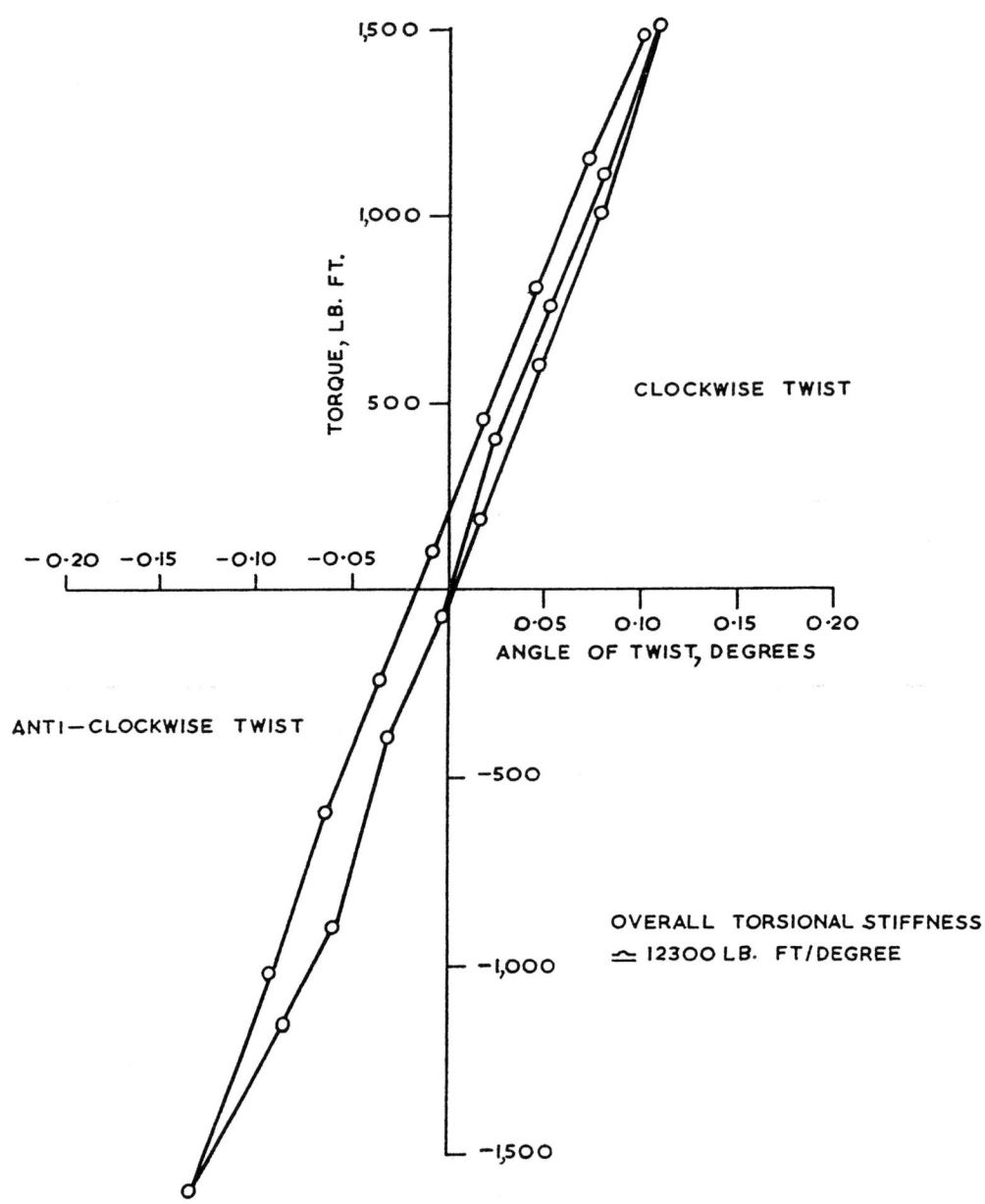

Overall twist of the complete vehicle. Torque was applied at the front and rear wheels.

After 70 passes, the front licence plate was covered but not obscured completely and there was a considerable accumulation on the wheels.

At the completion of the test, i.e., 100 passes, there had been no penetration into the luggage compartment and only a very slight influx into the passenger compartment. The front of the vehicle had the least accumulation with the headlights remaining free from dust throughout the test (see Fig. 3.12). Considerable build-up of dust was observed on the side windows and on the whole of the rear of the vehicle from just above the rear window (see Figs. 3.13 and 3.14). In spite of the overall liberal coverage in the engine compartment, nothing had penetrated past the air filter and the engine was unaffected (see Fig. 3.15). All auxiliary equipment and brakes functioned satisfactorily throughout the test.

When the engine was stripped for final inspection, it was found that a small amount of dust had accumulated within the clutch assembly.

(b) *Water*

After the first run at 15 m.p.h., there was a small amount of water deposited in the rear of the engine compartment. Spots of water reached both sides of the windscreen and both side windows on the second run. There was considerably more water in the engine compartment after the third

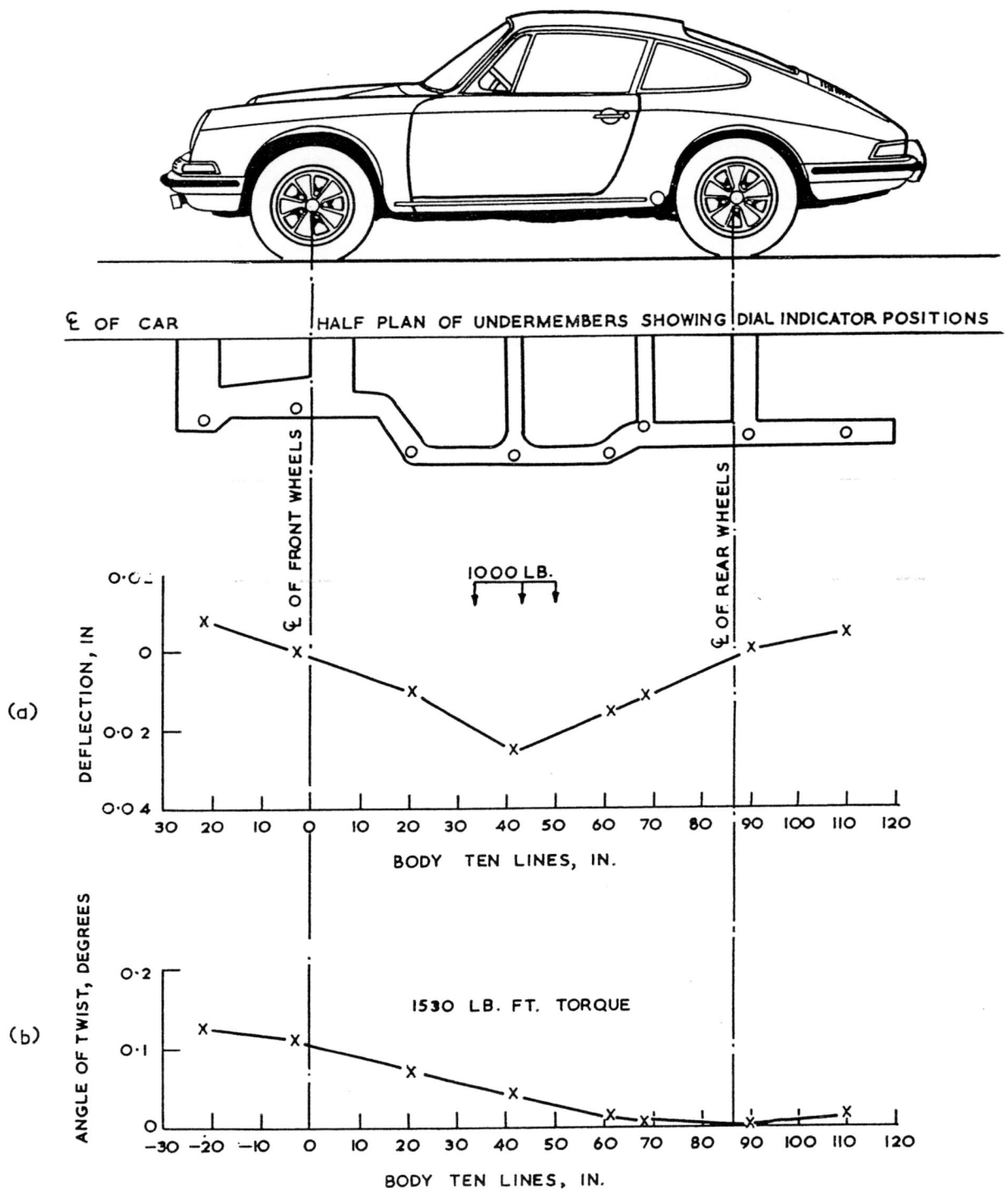

Structural stiffness.

(a) Bending deflection of the complete vehicle.

(b) Longitudinal distribution of twist.

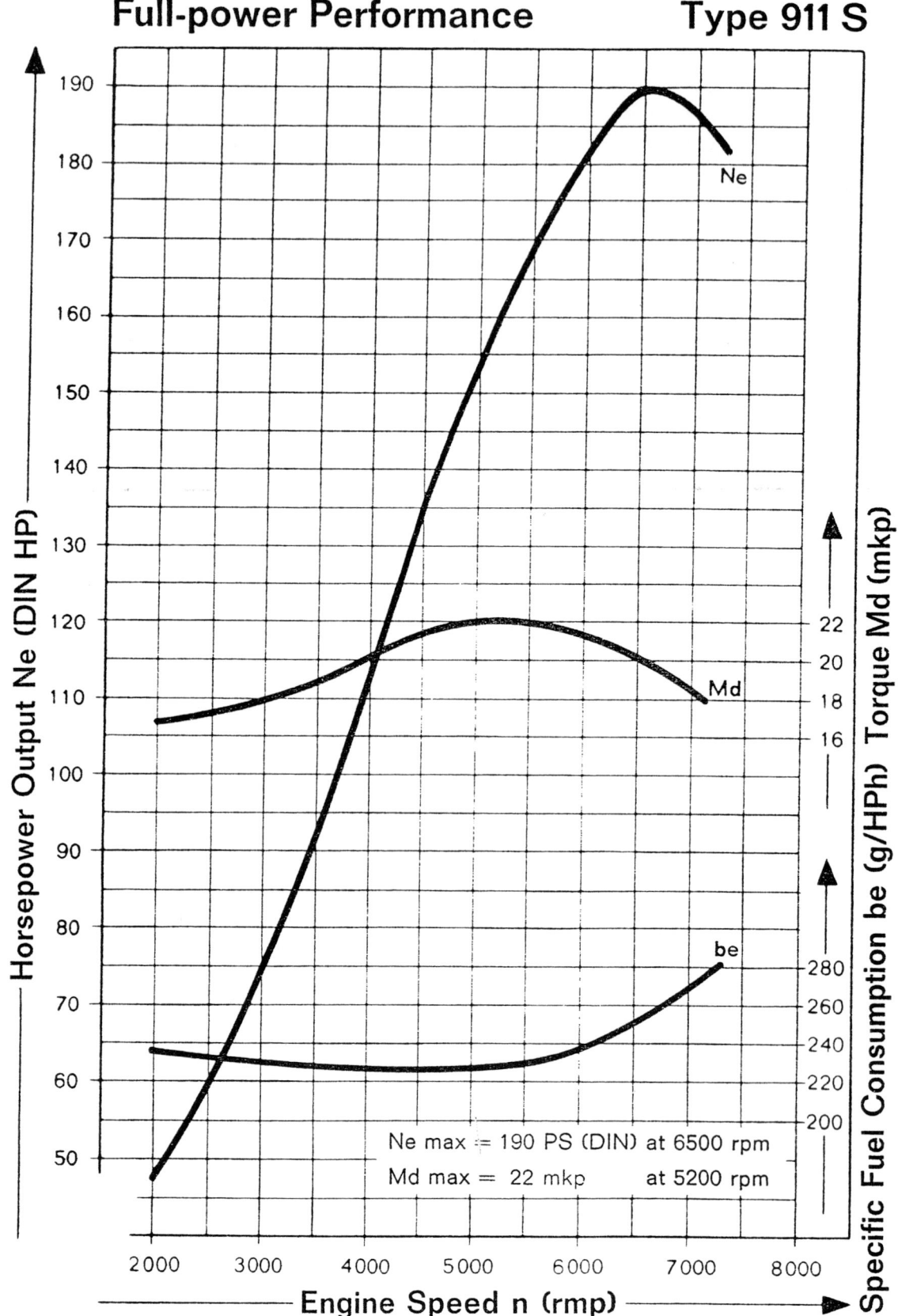

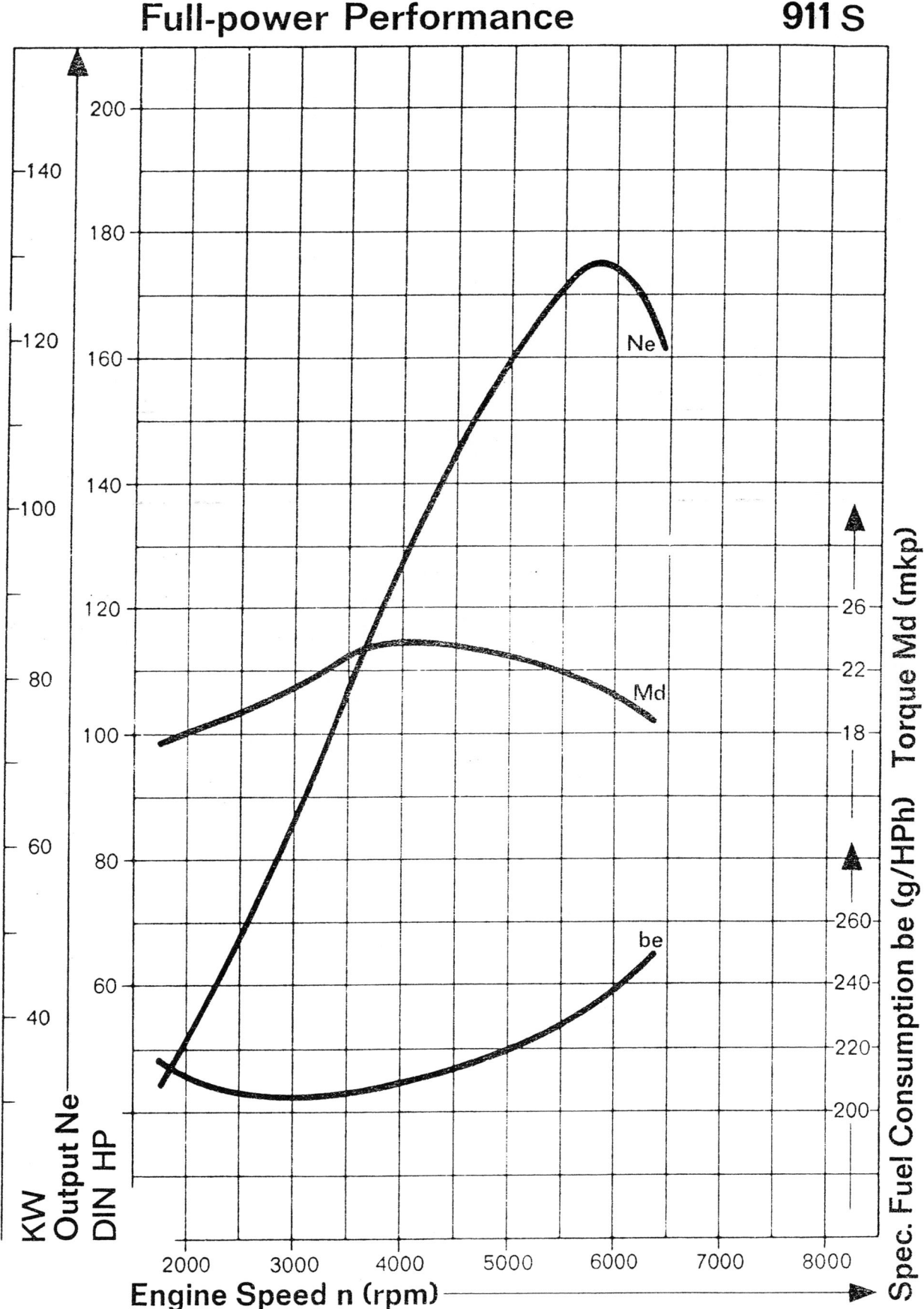

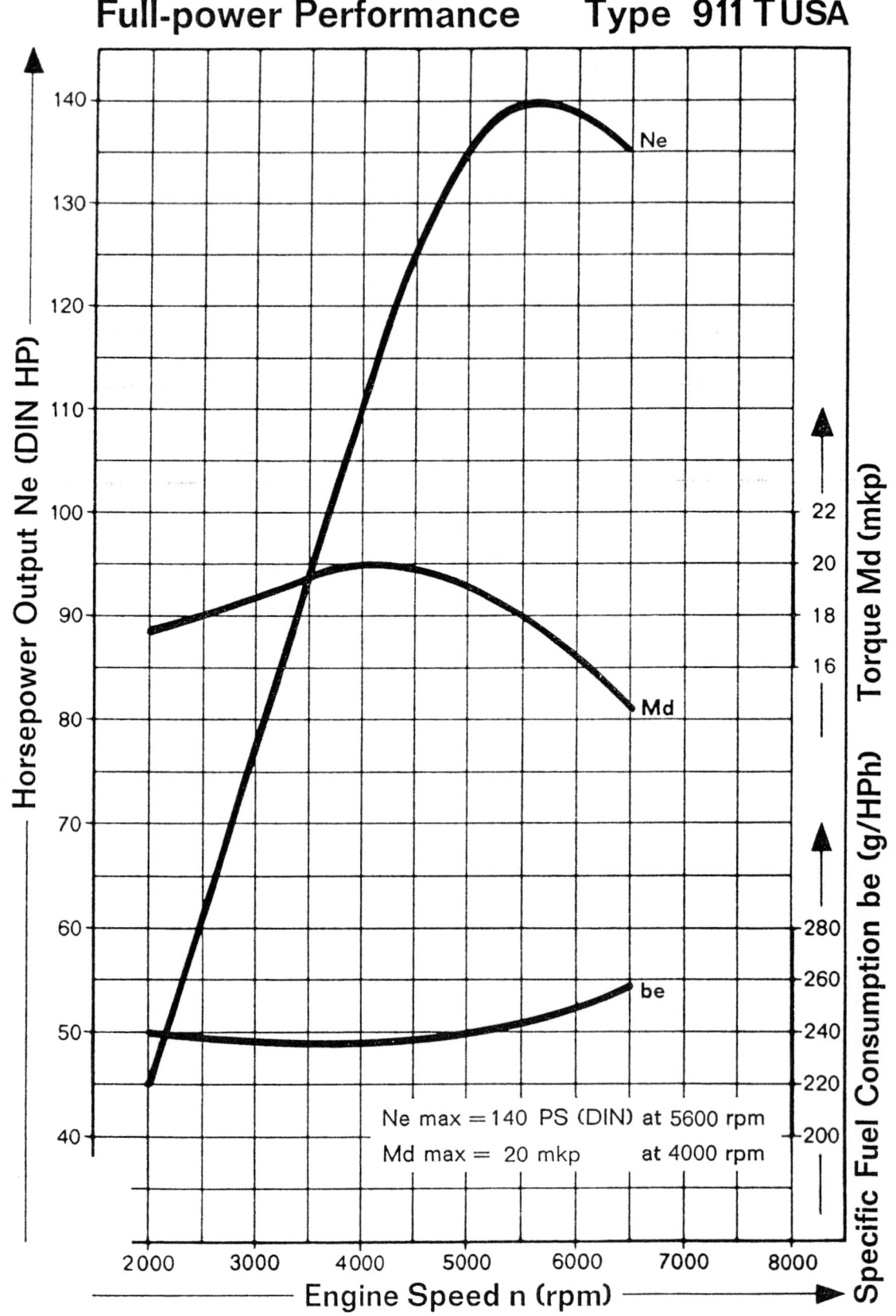

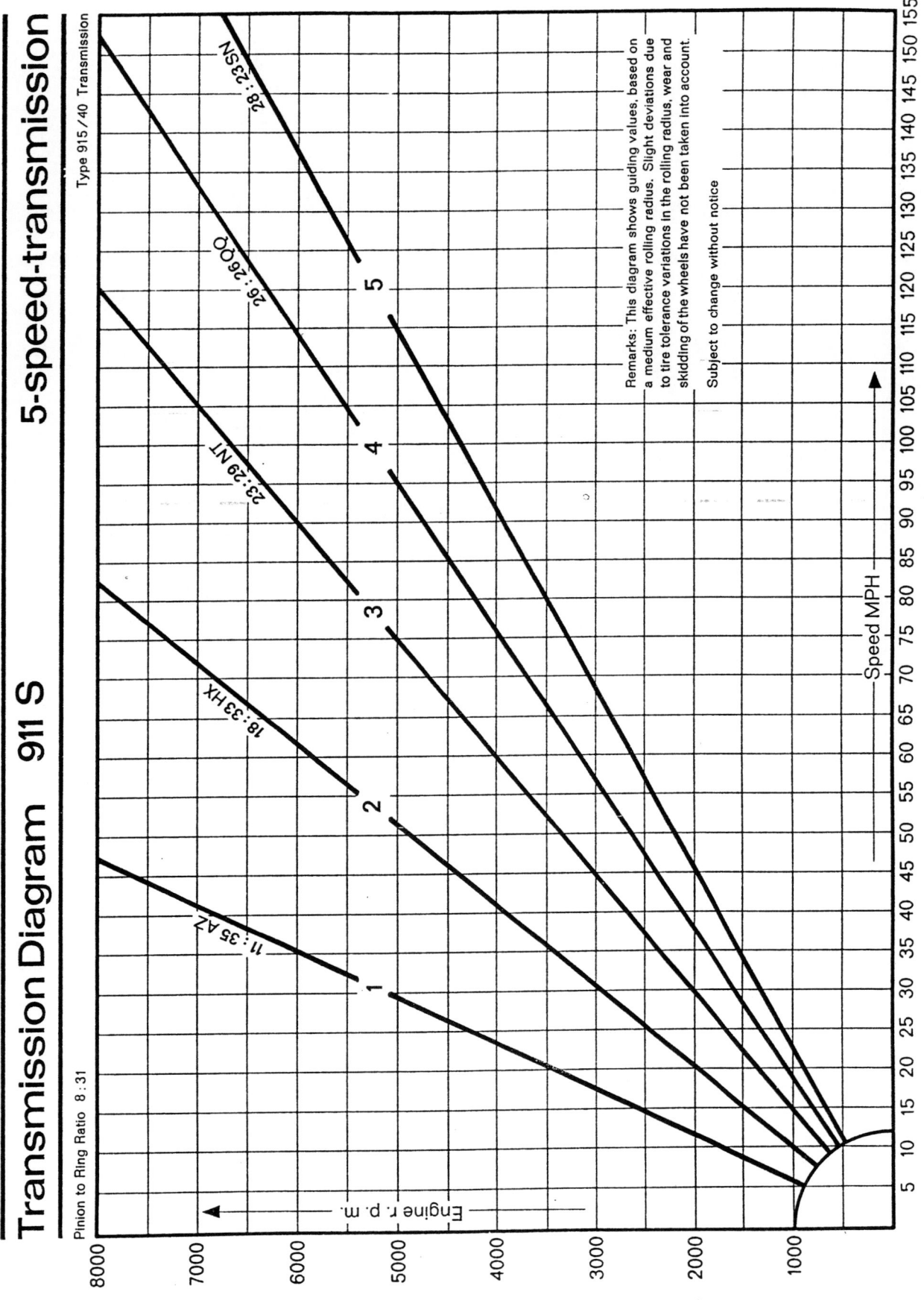

Performance on the order of an American Supercar but without the stigma of low cost

THIS YEAR all the Porsche 911 models get larger engines, thanks to a 4-mm bore increase that raises piston displacement from 1991 to 2195 cc. The results are power increases across the board: the T goes from 125 to 142 bhp, the E from 158 to 175 bhp and the all-out S from 190 to 200 bhp. The technically alert reader will notice that the S's power increase is the smallest: the new 2.2-liter version is less highly tuned than its predecessor for better general running and for meeting the ever-tightening emission regulations here in the U.S.; still it's remarkable that these laws can be met with an engine producing 91 bhp per liter or 1.49 bhp/cu in.

So, as the ads say, this year's T goes more like last year's E, this year's E more like last year's S, etc. But unfortunately the same can be said of prices: this year's T costs more like last year's E, and so forth. An inflating German economy and the upward revaluation of the Deutschmark mean higher prices for all German cars. Oh well, look at it this way: you're getting performance on the order of an American Supercar without the stigma of low cost.

But to the car. As impressive as the fact that it meets smog laws is the way the 911S runs: it idles smoothly at 800-1000 rpm and runs without any of the common symptoms of mixture leanness found in many of today's emission-control high-output engines at moderate speeds. It is necessary to juggle a hand throttle for cold starting, but the enrichment necessary for cold starting and running is an automatic function of the Bosch mechanical fuel injection.

The 911S, however, has serious drawbacks for driving in the speed-limited areas of the U.S.: though it will pull fairly smoothly at lower revs, it has very little torque until it gets to around 4500 rpm. And 50 mph (2300 rpm) is a practical minimum speed for 5th gear, for below that if you try to accelerate gearbox rattle sets in, probably excited by the engine's torsional vibrations. It lacks torque even for passing from 70 mph; one must shift down to get sparkling acceleration. The engine noise is also high; around town this can be embarrassing if you stand on it, and out on the highway it's always with you. But going up through the gears to the redline brings out noises that will warm hearts even of those accustomed to exotic V-12s. Glorious noises!

The 2.2 911S we tested fully lived up to Porsche's claims for it, getting from 0 to 60 mph in 7.3 sec and the stand-

54

ROAD TEST
2.2 PORSCHE 911S

SCALE: 10" DIVISIONS

PRICE
List price, east coast........$8750
List price, west coast........$8850
Price as tested..............$8850
Price as tested includes std equipment only (radial tires, alloy wheels, 5-speed gearbox, etc.) plus dealer prep

IMPORTER
Porsche Audi Div, VW of America
600 Sylvan Ave.
Englewood Cliffs, N.J. 07631

ENGINE
Type.....................flat 6, sohc
Bore x stroke, mm.....84.0 x 66.0
  Equivalent in........3.31 x 2.60
Displacement, cc/cu in..2195/134
Compression ratio............9.8:1
Bhp @ rpm...........200 @ 6500
  Equivalent mph..............140
Torque @ rpm........164 @ 5200
  Equivalent mph..............112
Fuel injection...Bosch mechanical
Type fuel required........premium
Emission control.....fuel injection

DRIVE TRAIN
Transmission.........5-sp manual
Gear ratios: 5th (0.758)....3.36:1
  4th (0.926)..............4.10:1
  3rd (1.22)...............5.38:1
  2nd (1.78)...............7.88:1
  1st (3.09)..............13.65:1
Final drive ratio...........4.43:1

CHASSIS & BODY
Layout......rear engine/rear drive
Body/frame.............unit steel
Brake type: vented disc, 11.1 in. front, 11.4-in. rear, vacuum assisted
  Swept area, sq in..........500
Wheels........alloy spoke, 15 x 6J
Tires......Michelin XVR 185/70-15
Steering type........rack & pinion
  Overall ratio...............17.8:1
  Turns, lock-to-lock..........3.1
  Turning circle, ft...........32.5
Front suspension: MacPherson struts, lower arms, torsion bars, tube shocks, anti-roll bar
Rear suspension: semi-trailing arms, torsion bars, tube shocks, anti-roll bar

ACCOMMODATION
Seating capacity, persons...2 + 2
Seat width, front/rear
                 .....2x21.0/2x14.5
Head room, front/rear...37.5/32.5
Seat back adjustment, degrees..75
Driver comfort rating (scale of 100):
  Driver 69 in. tall............90
  Driver 72 in. tall............85
  Driver 75 in. tall............70

INSTRUMENTATION
Instruments: 150-mph speedo, 8000-rpm tach, oil press, oil temp, oil level, fuel level, clock
Warning lights: generator, brake system, high beam, directionals, hazard flasher.

MAINTENANCE
Service intervals, mi:
  Oil change................6000
  Filter change.............6000
  Chassis lube..............none
  Minor tuneup..............6000
  Major tuneup..............6000
Warranty, mo/mi........24/24,000

GENERAL
Curb weight, lb..............2390
Test weight..................2640
Weight distribution (with driver), front/rear, %....43/57
Wheelbase, in................89.5
Track, front/rear.......53.8/53.0
Overall length..............163.9
  Width....................63.4
  Height...................52.0
Ground clearance.............5.9
Overhang, front/rear....35.0/39.4
Usable trunk space, cu ft......6.0
Fuel tank capacity, U.S. gal...16.4

CALCULATED DATA
Lb/bhp (test weight)..........13.2
Mph/1000 rpm (5th gear)....21.6
Engine revs/mi (60 mph)....2790
Engine speed @ 70 mph....3250
Piston travel, ft/mi..........1210
Cu ft/ton mi (4th gear).......100
R&T wear index...............34
R&T steering index..........1.01
Brake swept area sq in/ton....380

ROAD TEST RESULTS

ACCELERATION
Time to distance, sec:
  0-100 ft....................3.1
  0-250 ft....................5.2
  0-500 ft....................8.0
  0-750 ft...................10.3
  0-1000 ft..................12.5
  0-1320 ft (¼ mi)...........14.9
Speed at end of ¼ mi, mph...88.5
Time to speed, sec:
  0-30 mph....................2.6
  0-40 mph....................4.1
  0-50 mph....................5.6
  0-60 mph....................7.3
  0-70 mph....................9.8
  0-80 mph...................12.4
  0-100 mph..................19.7
Passing exposure time, sec:
  To pass car going 50 mph....4.0

FUEL CONSUMPTION
Normal driving, mpg.........15.0
Cruising range, mi...........245

SPEEDS IN GEARS
5th gear (6700 rpm).........144
  4th (7300).................129
  3rd (7300)..................97
  2nd (7300)..................65
  1st (7300)..................38

BRAKES
Panic stop from 80 mph:
  Max. deceleration rate, % g..84
  Stopping distance, ft........310
  Control..............very good
Fade test: percent increase in pedal effort to maintain 50%-g deceleration rate in 6 stops from 60 mph...................nil
Parking: Hold 30% grade?....yes
Overall brake rating....very good

SPEEDOMETER ERROR
30 mph indicated is actually...29.1
  40 mph.....................38.3
  60 mph.....................56.8
  70 mph.....................66.1
  80 mph.....................75.3
  100 mph....................93.7
Odometer, 10.0 mi............9.6

ACCELERATION & COASTING

Legend:
— Time to distance
– – Time to speed
⋯ Coasting

55

2.2 PORSCHE 911S

ing quarter in 14.9 before it had 1000 miles on its odometer. And it was the first Porsche we've tested to break the 15-sec quarter mile. The last S we tested, a 1967 model with 180 bhp, took 15.7 sec and did 0-60 in 8.1 sec.

Except for taller ratios in all but 1st gear, the Porsche transaxle unit remains unchanged: a beautiful piece of machinery that gives smooth, quick shifts and a "feel" that's quite good for linkage that has to reach so far to the rear. Our only objection is the shift pattern, which puts 1st over to the left and back, and we object to it because 1st gear seems to be needed so often—much more often than 5th, which in most 5-speeds is the out-of-the-way notch.

Since Porsche stretched the wheelbase of the 911 by over two inches and made available the remarkable Michelin XVR tire, the 911 has become our standard of how a GT should handle. This is a car that can be driven routinely and unobtrusively at cornering speeds that would have most good-handling cars scrabbling for traction. The steering, which is both quick and light, transmits every message the front tires generate—some drivers say too much so, as a certain bump-steer effect is noticed in hard cornering over bumps or dips—and makes fast driving over winding roads positively an ecstatic experience. Final oversteer, an inevitability with the 57% rearward weight bias of this car, is still there, but only a very foolhardy or a highly capable driver will ever discover it; the former will be in trouble, as he would in exceeding any car's limits, and the latter will enjoy it and use it to his advantage.

The 911's already good disc brakes are larger this year, having been increased from 9.25-in. front and 9.57-in. rear disc diameter to 11.1 front, 11.4 rear. These are marvelous brakes for repeated hard use and our standard fade test, designed as a simulation of severe but not outlandish use of brakes, was mere child's play for a system designed to cope with the 911S's 144-mph performance. Their behavior in our panic stop test was less exemplary: proportioning of front-rear brake effectiveness is such that the front wheels tend to lock up readily; this is good for stability but the maximum deceleration rate (84% g) achieved is not outstanding, especially with so much tire on the road.

Porsche shows the way to do it when it comes to controls and seating. There are the two steering-column stalks that allow one to operate windshield wipers and washers (this year one wiper speed gives intermittent wiping), directional signals, headlight dimming and flashing, all without looking away from the job of driving. The instruments are complete, decidedly businesslike and readable, and the seats are magnificent. There's occasional seating for two in the rear, for small children or for a short run with two adults.

A delicious "thunk" (is that the right word, Detroit?) when the doors are slammed, a nice rubber flap that comes out to protect the front fender from errant gasoline fillers, the carpeted trunk, etc., remind one of the great price tag of a Porsche. But things like the chronic wind leaks around the doors' leading edges, and rattles and squeaks that Porsches didn't have a few years ago, make us wonder if perhaps the little factory in Stuttgart-Zuffenhausen isn't cranking out too many cars and making too many annual changes to build them "the way they used to." A more positive note concerns the warranty: unlike other manufacturers who are generally reducing their warranties, Porsche this year has increased it to 24 months or 24,000 miles.

The 911S, exciting though it is, is not the right car for use in America—unless one lives in a state without open-road speed limits. The S just frustrates its poor driver most of the time in everyday driving, crying to be run up to its redline through the gears (do that in 2nd gear and you're at the speed limit in California) or cruised at 130-plus mph, and gives away a lot in low-speed performance to get its brilliant upper range, not to mention the extra cost. Since the 911T is also a bit stronger this year, and just as tractable as before, we recommend it as the best Porsche for all-around use—and a great car it is.

COMPARISON DATA	Porsche 911S	Corvette 427	Ferrari 330 GTS
List price	$8850	$6082	$14,900
Curb weight, lb	2390	3260	3415
0-60 mph, sec	7.3	6.1	6.9
Standing ¼-mi	14.9	14.3	14.9
Speed at end	88.5	98	95
Panic stop from 80 mph, % g	84	74	74
Fade in 6 stops from 60 mph, %	nil	nil	nil
R&T wear index	34	58	34
R&T steering index	1.01	1.11	1.03
Fuel economy, mpg	21.7	10.0	12.5

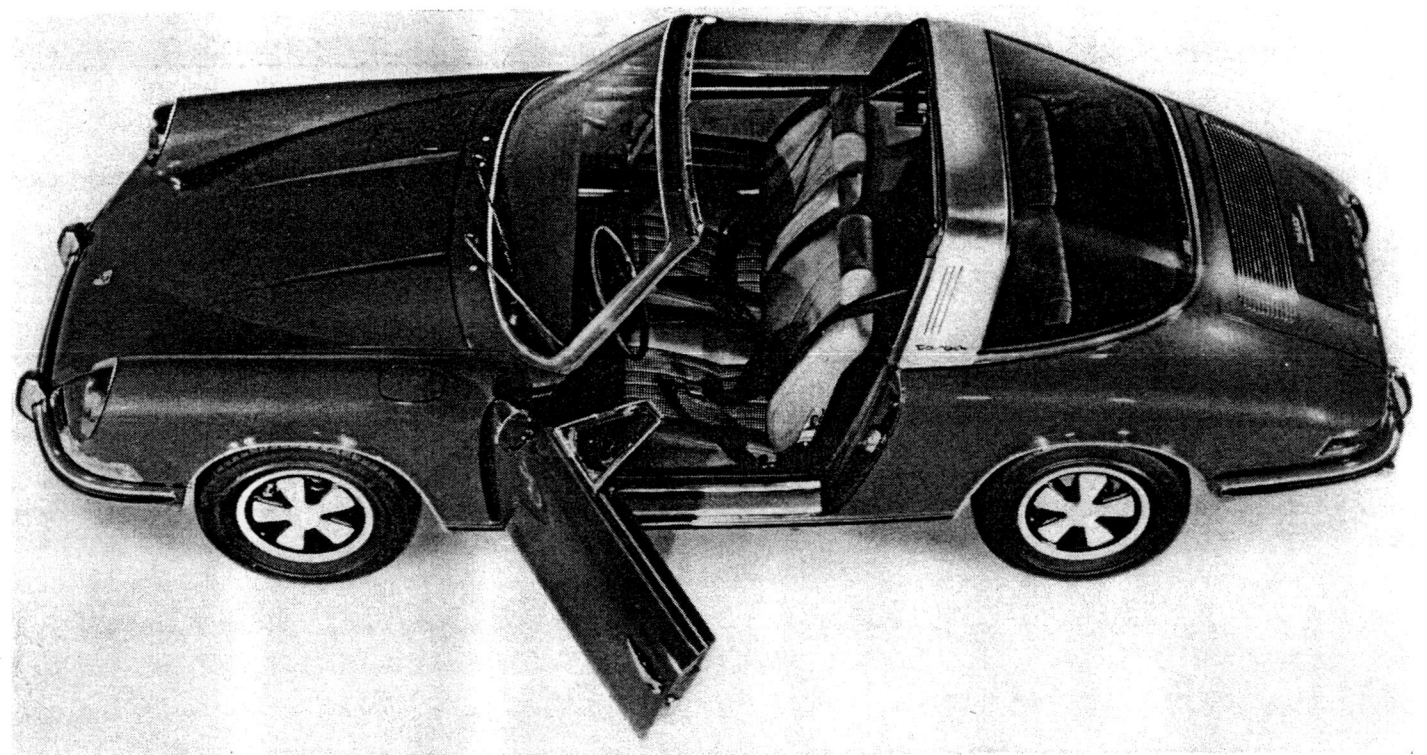

All Targas for 1969, whether 912, 911T, 911E or 911S, carry new fluting in the stainless-steel rollbar and a fixed, electrically heated rear window. This is a 911T with the new "comfort group" option that includes 14-in. alloy wheels and self-leveling.

PORSCHE LINEUP FOR '69

For an outfit that supposedly doesn't believe in the annual model change, Porsche still manages to come up with some significant news every year. For 1969 the painful condition in which they had to build a different model lineup for the U.S. has been cured and once again Porsche models for the whole world are alike except for such details as headlights and the difference between metric and English-reading instruments.

The 912 is continued, but 1969 will be the last year for it. Any dimensional changes described below will also apply to it.

Next in the heirarchy is the 911T, a model that was withheld from the U.S. market for about a year after its introduction. It carries a milder version of the 2-liter 6-cyl engine, rated at 125 bhp at 5500 rpm and using two triple-throat Weber carburetors. The 4-speed gearbox is standard, Sportomatic optional. Air pumps are not used on either 912 or 911T for emission control.

Replacing the regular 911 is the 911E, which is similar in valve timing and other details to the previous 911 but has a new fuel injection system that not only gives 12 more bhp (150 at 6500 rpm) but also controls exhaust emissions. The injection system is basically that of the sports prototype Porsches, consisting of a double-row, six-element mechanical pump between the two cylinder banks and driven by a toothed belt from the left camshaft. Fuel comes from the tank via an electric feed pump and an inline filter; with the pistons of the injection metering unit in the injection pump the fuel is sent into the injection tubes at a pressure of 220-265 psi, which pressure opens the valves out at the ports.

An air cleaner and noise damper unit (not shown) is held to each set of three ram-length intake pipes by over-center clips. Rotating throttle plates are in the pipes and are both interconnected and connected to the mixture control lever of the injection pump by mechanical linkage.

There's good news also for the drivers who have had troubles with their spark plugs sooting up: a high-voltage, capacitor discharge ignition system is now standard on the 911E and 911S.

Much to the delight of those who want a really fast car (even if it can't be driven fast legally in most of this country), the 911S is back, and with more horses to boot. Also carrying the new fuel injection system, and the usual wilder valve timing and higher compression ratio, the S now develops 195 bhp at 6800 rpm *and* meets the emission laws! Who said it couldn't be done?—it just takes time, especially for a small company like Porsche. (As an aside, we also understand that the Alfa 1750 will have injection when it hits our market.) The new S also has better torque at low speeds and better fuel economy, say the Porsche engineers. The S will be available only with the 5-speed manual gearbox.

The wheelbase has been lengthened by 2.2 in. on all models, mainly to improve the weight distribution on the 6-cyl models. The actual change is from 40/60 percent front/rear, to 42/58.

The 911S dash (with km/h speedo) showing its new steering-wheel hub and controls for the improved heating & venting.

PORSCHE 911T SPORTOMATIC

The semi-automatic transmission and mild engine make a very satisfying combination

THERE IS NO such thing as a non-sporting Porsche. But now that the 911 comes with a choice of three engines and three transmissions, some 911s are more sporting than others and the factory would admit that a 911T with Sportomatic is the least sporting model in the line.

This is far from being all bad. Because this is the first full test of the 911T since the engine grew from 2 to 2.2 liters, some review is in order. The current 911T uses two Zenith carburetors while the more expensive 911E and S have Bosch mechanical fuel injection. The T's compression ratio is 8.6:1 compared to 9.1:1 and 9.8:1. There are differences in camshaft timing as well and the T is rated at 142 bhp as against 175 and 200. On the good side, the T's peak power comes at 5800 rpm, the E needs 6200 and the S goes all the way to 6500. The more powerful versions have more power and torque up through the rev range, but not at the low end; it's safe to say that in most road situations you'd never be aware of either a lack of power or a deficiency between the T and the E or S. Power at everyday speeds is more useful and means more than power in the catalog.

The intangible virtues still spell Porsche. The 911T has that deep, raspy idle and the competitive howl at speed. There's a trace of roughness at low rpm, just enough to remind the driver and spectators that this is a sporting engine making higher-than-average demands on the operator's skill.

The transmission requires a definition of terms. The popular phrase is semi-automatic transmission and the popular phrase is right. There is nothing whatsoever automatic about the gearbox, though—it's the normal 4-speed Porsche unit. The difference is that the Sportomatic uses a torque converter and an automatic clutch. It's a manual clutch, if you'll pardon the double pun. Grab the gearshift knob and you activate a micro-switch that disengages the clutch via a vacuum servo. While the clutch is disengaged, you move the lever to whatever gear you want, just as with any manual transmission.

The torque converter is the normal power connection. The

PORSCHE 911T SPORTOMATIC

clutch is there to provide for shifting, by letting the input shaft spin freely when the gears are being moved from one place to another. With a gear selected and the knob released, the converter multiplies torque and allows the car to be stopped without declutching, in this form being just like an automatic transmission.

After the first block, driving the Sportomatic is easy, especially for those who drive a fully automatic transmission regularly. Allow one clumsy stab for the clutch pedal that isn't there and then shifting by hand alone quickly becomes a habit. The shifting sequence isn't quite like that of a standard transmission. This is a loose converter and allows the engine to speed up a few hundred rpm as the throttle is opened even at high speeds. This increases the power available from the engine at a given road speed and especially from a standstill. With the engine free to speed up, starts can easily be made in second gear and slow traffic negotiated in fourth gear without forcing the engine to labor. You can start in second, accelerate to 35 or 40 mph and drop into fourth.

The Sportomatic is like a standard 4-speed transmission in that anybody can operate one but it takes skill to operate it properly. The Sportomatic lends itself to sporty techniques. You can downshift, double-clutch, throw quick upshifts—all the techniques that make transmissions fun. And it takes some practice, coordinating throttle and clutch hand. Few owners of standard Porsches will be impressed by this but the Sportomatic owner can hold his head up at club meetings.

There is, at the same time, some loss of performance. This is due in part to the presence of the torque converter and part to the difference in gear ratios. The foot-clutch gearbox for the 911T has ratios of 3.09/1.63/1.04/0.76, 4.43 final drive.

ROAD TEST PORSCHE 911T SPORTOMATIC

SCALE: 10" DIVISIONS

PRICE
List price, west coast.......$6595
Price as tested.............$7763
Price as tested includes Sportomatic transmission ($315), appearance group ($170) cast alloy wheels ($375), AM-FM radio ($195) tinted glass ($65) dealer prep ($48)

IMPORTER
Porsche Audi Div., VW of America
600 Sylvan Ave.
Englewood Cliffs, N.J. 07632

ENGINE
Type.....................sohc H6
Bore x stroke, mm.....84.0 x 66.0
  Equivalent in.........3.31 x 2.60
Displacement, cc/cu in...2195/134
Compression ratio............9.8:1
Bhp @ rpm...........142 @ 5800
  Equivalent mph..............122
Torque @ rpm, lb-ft..148 @ 4200
  Equivalent mph...............87
Carburetion...2 Zenith 40TIN (3V)
Type fuel required.......premium
Emission control.....engine mods

DRIVE TRAIN
Transmission............4-speed semi-automatic
Gear ratios: 4th (0.86).....3.31:1
  3rd (1.13)................4.36:1
  2nd (1.55)................5.98:1
  1st (2.40)................9.26:1
  1st (2.40 x 2.15).......19.90:1
Final drive ratio..........3.86:1

CHASSIS & BODY
Layout.....rear engine/rear drive
Body/frame............unit steel
Brake type: 11.1-in. disc front, 11.1-in. disc rear
  Swept area, sq in.........500
Wheels.......alloy spoke, 14 x 5.5
Tires.....Michelin XAS 185HR-14
Steering type.......rack & pinion
  Overall ratio............17.8:1
  Turns, lock-to-lock..........3.1
  Turning circle, ft..........32.5
Front suspension: MacPherson struts, lower arms, torsion bars, tube shocks, anti-roll bar
Rear suspension: semi-trailing arms, torsion bars, tube shocks, anti-roll bar

ACCOMMODATION
Seating capacity, persons....2+2
Seat width, front/rear 2 x 21/2 x 14
Head room, front/rear...37.5/32.5
Seat back adjustment, degrees..75

INSTRUMENTATION
Instruments: 150-mph speedo, 8000-rpm tach, oil pressure, oil temp, oil level, fuel level, clock
Warning lights: generator, brake system, high beam, directionals

MAINTENANCE
Service intervals, mi:
  Oil change................6000
  Filter change.............6000
  Chassis lube..............none
  Tuneup...................6000
Warranty, mo/mi......24/24,000

RELIABILITY
From R&T Owner Surveys the average number of trouble areas for all models surveyed is 10.6. As owners of earlier model Porsche 911 reported 8 trouble areas, we expect reliability of the Porsche 911T to be better than average

GENERAL
Curb weight, lb............2390
Test weight.................2700
Weight distribution (with driver), front/rear, %....43/57
Wheelbase, in..............89.5
Track, front/rear........53.8/53.0
Overall length.............163.9
Width......................63.4
Height.....................52.0
Ground clearance............5.9
Overhang, front/rear....35.0/39.4
Usable trunk space, cu ft......6.0
Fuel tank capacity, U.S. gal...16.4

CALCULATED DATA
Lb/bhp (test weight).........19.0
Mph/1000 rpm (4th gear).....20.3
Engine revs/mi (60 mph).....2950
Piston travel, ft/mi..........1277
R & T steering index.........1.01
Brake swept area sq in/ton....370

Sportomatic has 2.40 (multiplied by the 2.15 of the torque converter)/1.55/1.13 and 0.86 with 3.86 final drive. Sporto's overall ratios are all higher, but the converter gives a low starting ratio. While second and third are closer together, and the final gearing about the same. The gearbox and type of clutch must be considered as complete units, and here's how they compare:

	911 T Manual	Sportomatic
0-60 mph	8.1 sec	9.1 sec
0-100	23.7 sec	27.0 sec
Standing ¼-mi	16.0 sec @ 85 mph	17.2 sec @ 83 mph
mpg	21.0	19.8

The standard transmission and clutch get the 911T off the mark quicker. And the mpg figure shows that the converter is using some fuel, even with 2nd-gear starts.

In that connection, we did a non-standard test, and timed the test car from 0-40 mph using second gear only, and with a first-gear start. First did make a difference, as the time dropped from 5.4 sec to 4.9. There are scores of cars on the

ROAD TEST RESULTS

ACCELERATION
Time to distance, sec:
- 0-100 ft ... 3.5
- 0-250 ft ... 5.6
- 0-500 ft ... 9.0
- 0-750 ft ... 11.8
- 0-1000 ft ... 14.5
- 0-1320 ft (¼ mi) ... 17.2

Speed at end of ¼ mi, mph ... 83
Time to speed, sec:
- 0-30 mph ... 3.4
- 0-40 mph ... 4.7
- 0-50 mph ... 6.8
- 0-60 mph ... 9.1
- 0-70 mph ... 11.9
- 0-80 mph ... 15.9
- 0-100 mph ... 27.0

Passing exposure time, sec:
To pass car going 50 mph ... 5.5

FUEL CONSUMPTION
- Normal driving, mpg ... 19.8
- Cruising range, mi ... 320

SPEEDS IN GEARS
- 4th gear (5800 rpm) ... 122
- 3rd (6300) ... 101
- 2nd (6300) ... 72
- 1st (6300) ... 44

BRAKES
Panic stop from 80 mph:
- Max. deceleration rate, % g ... 77
- Stopping distance, ft ... 312
- Control ... good
- Pedal effort for 50%-g stop, lb ... 40

Fade test: percent increase in pedal effort to maintain 50%-g deceleration rate in 6 stops from 60 mph ... nil
Parking: Hold 30% grade? ... yes
Overall brake rating ... very good

HANDLING
- Speed on 100-ft radius, mph ... 34.2
- Lateral acceleration, % g ... 0.782

SPEEDOMETER ERROR
- 30 mph indicated is actually ... 29.0
- 40 mph ... 38.0
- 50 mph ... 48.0
- 60 mph ... 57.0
- 70 mph ... 64.0
- 80 mph ... 74.0
- 100 mph ... 93.0
- Odometer, 10.0 mi ... 9.7

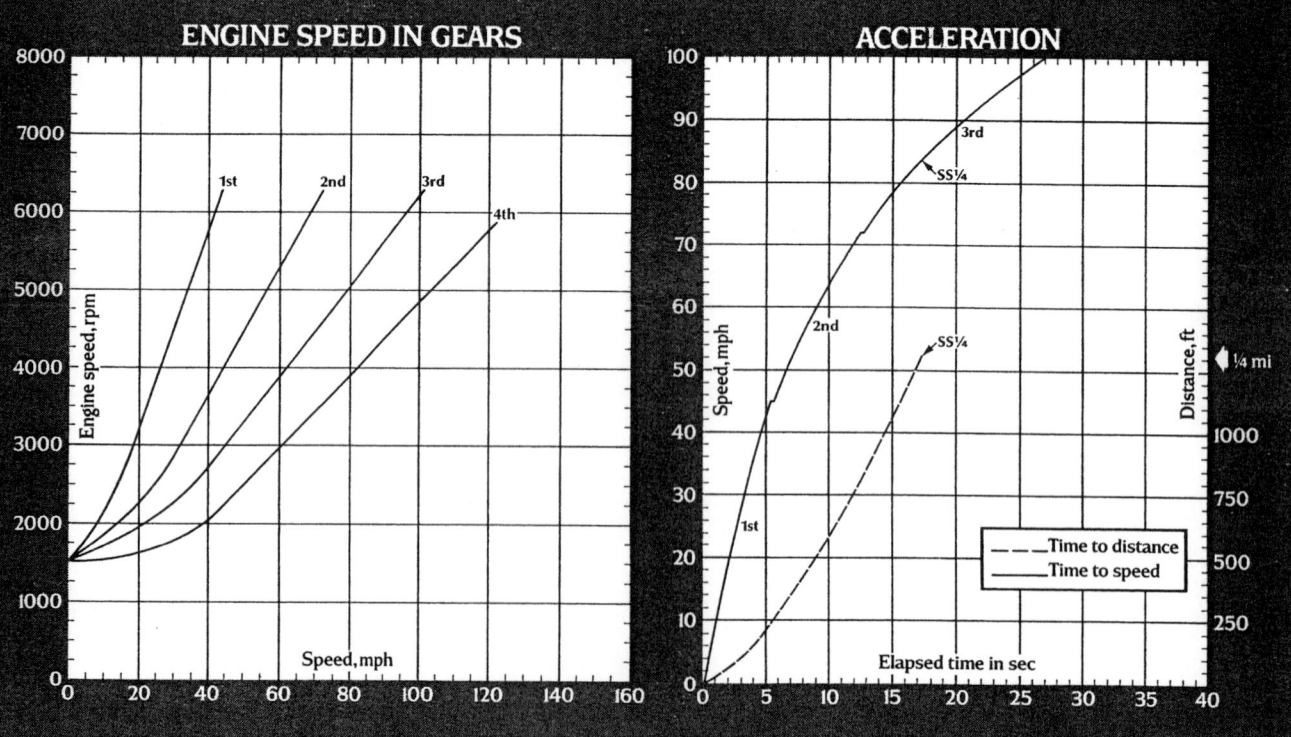

PORSCHE 911T SPORTOMATIC

market which take longer than 5.4, so it's no hardship, but we wondered just what the loss in performance was.

We are inclined to consider the Sportomatic an excellent answer to a question that hasn't been asked. In its favor, it detracts only slightly from the pleasures of driving. Maybe not at all; it is fun to develop any skill. There is a small loss in performance and efficiency but not much.

The benefits are no more overwhelming. Your left foot can stay planted on the floor, true. But there are only a few traffic situations, say, crawling through town in the rush hour, where the exertion of clutch pedal effort becomes annoying or tiring. And the transmission doesn't shift itself, ever. It is not automatic and thus doesn't lend itself to effortless driving. Win a little, gain a little. The 911T buyer will just have to decide whether or not the reduction in effort is worth $316 extra.

The 911T comes with what is also the standard suspension or perhaps it's the absence of the stiffer suspension installed with the 911S engines. The test car was fitted with nice, fat Michelin XAS 185HR tires. A good combination. The ride is very pleasant, firm without the taut jiggle of the 911S, and the tires develop plenty of grip for a good reading on the skid pad and a secure feeling on the road.

The softening of the suspension, in particular the rear, minimizes the traditional oversteer. Driven hard, there's a shade of understeer right up to cornering speeds high enough to lift the inside front tire—but the tail still comes out finally.

A warning: The Sportomatic can have a clutch pedal, in the proper use of the term, if you're not prepared. Going around a lefthand turn, if you brace yourself with your right foot and splay your knee far enough, it hits the gearshift and the pressure activates the switch, leading to a disengaged (and racing) engine. A baffling phenomenon for a split second and an embarrassment if there's someone else in the car.

Under more normal circumstances, the Porsche had three handling quirks. One was simply a tendency to hunt, making tiny darting motions from straight ahead. It's not enough to be considered tricky but it calls for constant vigilance.

The second is a transition from under to oversteer when the throttle is closed. As the weight shifts back, it can hang the rear wheels out. Again, no real cause for alarm but for attention. The instinctive reaction to a sudden change in situation, a curve that was tighter than it looked, for example, or something in the road, is to lift off. And the reversal of cornering attitude adds a dimension to whatever it was that caused you to lift. Some care is required when going fast over unfamiliar roads.

When cornering hard across a dip, the car developed a yaw. That is, the body pivots around its center. As it does, the driver steers with it. This doesn't call for any correction, really, but the same amount of steering effort that was holding the car on its line suddenly becomes enough effort to move the wheel an inch or two. This seems to be more a result of the low friction in the Porsche's steering, which doesn't damp out the reaction of the road wheels. Not desirable in an ordinary passenger car, perhaps, but acceptable—maybe even desirable—in a good sports car.

For the rest, it's pure Porsche: Excellent seats, instruments and controls, fine workmanship and finish flawed only by the windleak in the right door. All 911s seem to have this.

When we tested the 911S, we were impressed with the performance but put off by the lack of low-speed torque.

We said then that the 911T was the better choice for road use. We still think so.

AUTO TEST

PORSCHE CARRERA RS TOURING

Sensational, even by Porsche standards

AT-A-GLANCE: "Homologation special" which demand must make into a full production Porsche. Extraordinary performance, yet more tractable than other Porsches. Superb brakes, roadholding, traction and steering; but demands expert driving more than other cars of similar performance. A classic whose speed makes its price more justifiable than is usual.

Without any particularly dramatic announcement, Porsche quietly presented the Carrera RS to the public at last autumn's Paris Motor Show. Boring out the 2,341 c.c. six-cylinder *Boxermotor*—as the Germans have it—of the 911 series by 6mm put the principal dimensions of the engine to 90×70.4mm, the capacity up to 2,687 c.c., maximum power to 210 bhp (DIN) at 6,300 rpm, and peak torque to 188 lb ft at 5,100 rpm. Five hundred cars were to be made in order to qualify the car's entry into Group 4 sports-car racing. Every one was ordered before it was built. So far as any Porsche enthusiast is concerned, it is hard to see how the factory can avoid making as many Carreras as possible. It is the fastest road-going Porsche and also, perhaps even more valuably, the most tractable.

Differences

The Carrera RS Touring is based on the previously fastest similar Porsche, the 911S, and uses much of the 911S equipment and specification. To put the Carrera's statistics into perspective, the 911S engine has the same compression ratio (8.5-to-1), maximum power of 190 bhp (DIN) at 6,500 rpm, and peak torque of 159 lb ft at 5,200 rpm. Actual differences in engine construction are limited to more heavily ribbed cylinder barrels (15 instead of 11 cooling ribs)—these barrels cannot be re-bored, understandably—slightly flatter-topped pistons, and altered ignition timing. The Bosch fuel-injection pumps have a suitably uprated output. Crankshaft, camshafts, valves, cylinder heads and valve timing are 911S; like its predecessors of late, the RS runs happily on normal 2-star 91-octane fuel. The same 7/31 (4.429-to-1) final drive and five-speed gearbox are used, but 4th and 5th ratios are a little higher; the use of 215/60 VR 15 in. Pirelli Cinturato CN36 tyres on 7 in. rims at the rear puts the calculated overall gearing up to 24.06 mph per 1,000 rpm. At the front (and on the spare) 185/70 VR 15 in. tyres are used on 6 in. rims. The same hefty sized anti-roll bar (0.59 in.) is fitted front and rear (front only on the 911S); a lighter forged aluminium alloy front sub-frame is employed, dampers are Bilstein at both ends, and the rear suspension is reinforced. The most obvious external difference is the dolphin-like dorsal spoiler which is part of the glass-fibre engine cover; the ordinary engine cover is available if specially ordered, but Porsche point out that it is no gimmick, improving rear adhesion above 100 mph, improving straight stability and actually lowering the drag coefficient of the body. Independent confirmation of that last claim was supplied by a road test in a German magazine which found that, using the standard engine cover lowered the maximum speed by 4½ mph.

There are variations in specification; the car tested is the Porsche Carrera RS Touring (code-numbered M472); there is the Carrera RS itself (M471); a third variation is listed, the Carrera RS Racing version (M491). By the usual removal of items like soundproofing, electric windows and so on, a claimed 250 lb is removed on the Carrera RS which is usually known unofficially in this country as the "lightweight".

Handling experiments on a wet MIRA circuit. The lefthand bend was entered at about maximum speed for the conditions. Initially accelerating in the corner to tighten the effective cornering line by breaking away the tail only made the car run wide; traction and adhesion of the rear is too good for the front, which loses grip. Therefore, a moment before this point the throttle has been released, upsetting the car's balance, breaking away the back tyres; the driver must be quick to catch the resulting slide, which begins sharply. The wheel-lifting is not nearly as alarming as it looks. Although the MIRA track surface is a very good one, it says much for both the car and the Pirelli tyres (here on standard pressures) that there is enough grip in the wet to generate such cornering forces

Traction is outstandingly good; note the nose-up attitude under heavy acceleration on this wet surface

Performance

As usual on current Porches, starting from cold is an uncharacteristically restrained business of lifting the rich mixture lever in between the seats, and turning over the engine, without any noticeable pressure on the organ accelerator pedal, whereupon the engine fires and slowly increases its tickover. Warming-up is very quick—one of the few advantages of the Porsche's engine-blown heater is felt here, in the very early delivery of heated air for demisting on a cold morning. With a warm power unit, starting is much more of an indication of what is to come—turn the key and the engine leaps into life with stirring alacrity, almost as if there is no flywheel at all—throttle response is more like a racing car than a roadgoing one. Press the clutch pedal, which needs a surprisingly low 30 lb effort, and engage first gear—the gearchange too is very light most of the time—and move off. One might expect to have to use high rpm and lots of clutchslip to get away. Nothing could be farther from the truth. More so than its smaller brothers, the Carrera will potter about contentedly for as long as you like, tick over reliably, and is appreciably more flexible than the others. We have a suspicion that it is also slightly quieter, though only a side-by-side test could decide the point.

So, you can drive out of built-up areas with no unseemly indication that you are in an unusual Porsche—apart perhaps, in the case of the test car, from the fin and heavy sign-writing along the sides. Get clear of restrictions and, for a beginning, put your foot down in, say, third gear; this gives you a little more time to appreciate exactly what happens.

Starting from below 20 mph, the car accelerates, but not excitingly. At 1,800 rpm it begins to pull acceptably, continuing unexceptionally to around 3,000 rpm. At 3,200 rpm the note of the always audible engine changes and the car shoots forward; at 4,500 a heartwarming deep growl begins and one feels an almost unbelievable further increase in the pressure of the seat on one's back which is vastly exhilarating, continuing as it does all the way to around 7,000 rpm. An ignition cut-out prevents one revving beyond 7,200 rpm, which is just as well, because the way the revs rise, especially in the lower gears, makes it all too easy to over-speed the engine.

At MIRA, the acceleration figures obtained were outstanding. After several experiments, we found that the clutch did not care for clutch-slipping starts; in an interesting mechanical example of being cruel to be kind, the safest way to get off the line was to rev to between 5,000 and 5,500 rpm, and to let the clutch in as if the pedal had suddenly become red-hot. Only then was it possible to break the exceptionally sure grip of the Cinturatos on the tarmac to produce wheelspin instead of clutchspin. Nevertheless, so quick was the car's getaway and so good its traction that the black marks continued for only a relatively short way. Once the wheels had gripped again, changing gear at around 6,750 rpm, one was in 1st for only a very short time; 2nd took one from 37 mph to 64 mph; 3rd to 93; 4th to 127; and a brief snatch of top gear just after 124 mph and the kilometre took the car to a clear 130 mph before we had to brake for the end of the straight. Times recorded on our electronic recorder confirmed the fact that this Porsche is one of the world's fastest road-going cars, at any rate at the more frequently used lower and middle ends of the speed scale. Thirty mph appeared in 2.1 sec; 50 in 4.6; 60 in 5.5; 80 in 9.6; the quarter-mile in 14.1; 100 in 15.0; 120 in 21.9; the kilometre in 25.4; and 130 in just over half a minute.

Aerodynamics lesson still visible half an hour after a wet motorway drive. Turbulence and what the makers say is an area of positive pressure deposits road filth behind the dorsal spoiler, in contrast to the relative cleanliness of the smoothly swept body in front and around the fin

We took it to Belgium for maximum speed runs where it recorded 149 mph both ways in good conditions. Unfortunately, we have not tested the 911S with the 2.4-litre engine, but the slightly better-than-specification 2.4 911E tested in *Autocar* of 25 November 1971 with 165 bhp at its disposal was 10 mph slower, got to 60 mph in 6.4 sec; the quarter-mile in 14.4; 100 in 17.2; and 120 in 1 sec longer than the Carrera took to reach 130. One knows, all current Porsches are quick, but the 2.7 car is appreciably quicker than the rest.

Perhaps the most valuable point about this performance is that, for all normal road-going purposes, so much of it is so easy to use. The gearchange is very good; it follows the Alfa Romeo pattern, with reverse opposite 5th, but unlike the Alfa it takes a little more learning for those unfamiliar with it, because not having the Alfa's spring-loading of the gearlever into one spot—neutral between 3rd and 4th—one is not at first quite so sure where one is sometimes. First and 2nd are a little remote from the driver; the nearest the beat-proof synchromesh comes to baulking is felt when a noticeably higher pressure is needed to complete a change; this happens so seldom that it takes one by surprise. Ratios are perfectly suited to the car.

Thanks to the increased flexibility, one is not gearchanging all the time on a give-and-take road. Properly used, the thrilling reserves of power make overtaking wonderfully quick and safe; one is on the wrong side of the road for the shortest possible time.

Another major reason for the readiness with which one uses the performance is found in the superb way the car puts all the power down on the road. No wasteful, attention—getting wheelspin and attendant slewing; it simply *goes*—and how. Leaving a slow corner is one of the greatest and most satisfying pleasures of Carrera driving. You can "put the boot in" that little bit earlier on the exit, the car rocketing up the straight with the back wheels apparently glued to the road. Obviously, one has to respect the risk of breaking away the back end in such circumstances in the wet, but it is still remarkable how little twitch there is and how much acceleration—provided you don't abruptly alter your right foot.

If one were to establish a comparative factor of maximum speed divided by size of a car's body, the Carrera RS would, so far as we know, lead the road-going list. It is only 13 ft 8 in. long and 5 ft 3½ in. wide; compare that with the 14½ ft and 5¾ ft of the Ferrari Daytona, or the 15 ft and 6 ft of the Aston Martin V8. The point about this comparison is that such relatively small overall size—and especially the width—make it so much easier to drive the Porsche quickly on many British roads (where it is safe to do so, of course).

As before, our fuel-flow meter is not compatible with fuel injection, and no figures are obtainable from the manufacturer, so that we are unable to publish any steady-speed fuel consumption table. Overall we recorded 16.7 mpg, slightly better than the 15.6 mpg returned by the 911E Road Test car. For reasons that will be understood by foregoing remarks, during its 2,600 odd miles with us, the Carrera

Rear accommodation is minimal for people and quite handy for extra luggage when the "seat" backs are folded down

63

AUTOTEST
PORSCHE CARRERA RS
TOURING...

rarely was driven by any staff member with much thought to economy; consumption varied mostly between 15 and 18mpg, though we did once see 20 mpg. Considering the performance—you could describe it as at least 4½-litres' worth from 2.7—such a thirst seems moderate. The test car had the ordinary 911S 13.6-gallon tank, which gave a restricted range at the high cruising speeds—120 mph—of which the car is capable; an 85-litre (18.7 gallons) plastic tank is available in Germany, but such tanks are not yet permitted in Britain. Some petrol pump attendants are sceptical about such a car running on 2-star fuel, and need reassurance.

Noise
The engine is dominant, as usual, when one is driving hard—the customary Porsche flat-six thrash that growls marvellously at mid-range as already described, rising to a unique, fairly subdued near-scream at the top end. Occasionally the test car disgraced itself with a loud backfire on the over-run. Gently driven, engine noise takes second place to the quite high level of bump-thump-induced road-roar that is generated over coarse concrete surfaces. We noticed some heterodying between 3,500 and 4,500 rpm. On a long journey one grows tired of the continuous drone behind. A slight increase in engine noise is noticed when the heater is turned to "hot". The transmission is often audible, clattering a little when pulling from low engine speeds, and also whining somewhat in all gears. There is some wind noise, mainly from around the front pillars, plus a little from behind.

Handling, ride and brakes
With only 41.2 per cent of the unladen weight on the front wheels, it is not surprising that the Carrera's steering is unusually light. Like all the rear-engined Porches it is a very relaxing car to manoeuvre for this reason. Possibly more so than the others, steering effort is directly proportional to cornering speed. As you corner faster, so the straightening pull on the steering wheel rim increases. There is, by other cars' standards, an unusually large amount of kick-back over any sort of unevenness. Correspondingly, feel is very good, assisted by the virtual lack of any stickiness or excess friction. Gearing is just right, 3.2 turns from lock to lock corresponding to a quite compact mean turning circle of 33½ ft diameter; the car is very swerveable, as any sports-car should be.

Straight line stability in still air even at maximum speed is good provided that the surface is smooth. On an uneven road there is a little wander, and side winds affect the car's progress a lot.

Steering load going up markedly with cornering speed, plus the combination of a lightly loaded front end; extremely good traction, and the great power of the engine combine to disguise to some extent the rear-heaviness of the car. Too much power in a bend merely increases the understeer induced by acceleration very noticeably. The best way to drive the Porsche round corners on public roads is also the only safe way in any case; assuming one can see and that all is clear, enter the bend no faster than is reasonable, begin to apply power in it, and then make the best use of the traction on the exit to accelerate away to great effect. Too early with the right foot does not often break the tail away except in slippery going, but merely makes the nose run wide. "Slow in, fast out" is the maxim.

So good is the roadholding of the Carrera RS on these remarkable Pirelli tyres in both dry and wet that very high cross-country averages can be achieved easily. The one and only catch remains. By sensible development—notably the replacement of the original very skittish swinging-axle rear suspension with a semi-trailing arm set up—the inherent dangers of the unavoidably imbalanced rear-engine design are largely avoided. The point at which a driver will run into difficulties is pushed so high that, for all normal purposes, the car is perfectly safe. But if, for whatever reason, a driver finds himself attempting a corner at too high a speed, and if he obeys his first instincts, which will probably be to decelerate, then the rear tyres can lose their grip so abruptly that it is difficult to hold the car out of a spin. Track experiments at MIRA revealed that, just before this point was reached, what felt to the driver like more than usual roll was partly the result of the inside front wheel lifting. Ride is appreciably better at high speed than at low, when it reacts quite sharply to some bumps. The usual rear-engine pitch is hardly present at all.

The brakes are superb, neither too light nor too heavy, which is remarkable nowadays when one sees that, as before, this latest Porsche still manages without any servo assistance. The pad material is a little dead at first, becoming more responsive as it is warmed; fade resistance is good. If one does have to brake really hard, it is comforting to know that the combination of rear-heaviness and beautiful braking balance is on your side; we achieved a best stop of just over 1g without any difficulty at all.

Engine room looks rather crowded at first sight. Note the various plates giving service information

Driving position
Few will quarrel with most aspects of Porsche interior design. The seat is ve nearly as good as a rally-type for holdin one in place, and can be adjusted to su both short and tall drivers. The 911 boc is a refreshingly good example of an ur common quality amongst very fast ca today; it has good vision all round with r stupid styling blind-spots caused by heav quarter panels. The windscreen wipe sweep an area of glass that suits righ hand-drive as well as left; they are a usual driven by a three-speed motor th gives 44, 64 or 86 sweeps per minute (w still think that it would be more useful replace the slowest speed with a hesita tion-wipe setting). The electric four-j washers give floods of water just whe you need it; their control is combined in good stalk on the column. The rear scree has a two-position heater element; or can clear either the top two-thirds or a of the glass. As explained earlier, the isn't too much Porsche, so that althoug one cannot see both ends, one has pretty good idea where they are. One ca see about 3in. of the fin in the insid mirror, but it doesn't block any vision tha is needed.

Pedals are well-arranged, providin good heel-and-toe facility; the action the throttle pedal is beautifully cor trived, which is as it should be with suc an engine. On a motorway, one finds it be to rest the unoccupied left foot betwee clutch and brake, since there isn't enoug room to the left of the clutch. The hanc brake works well and is handy. So are a other important minor controls, the ho perhaps a little too much so; it is easy sound it unintentionally.

Instruments are as on the 911S, fro left to right, a fuel *and* oil contents gaug oil temperature and pressure, 8,000 rp revcounter, speedometer with trip, and clock with a journey-start line on Manufacturers always seem to do an provide speedometers that, to the ignoran suggest a top speed far higher than the c will actually do; this Porsche must be th most modest car ever in this respec having a maximum reading only 1 mp (0.67 per cent) higher than its tru maximum speed. The revcounter is bang front of the driver and can easily be rea the speedometer on the other hand obscured between 70 to 130 mph by t steering wheel rim.

Ventilation is good, but the heated-a heating system with its engine-fan-induce blowing is almost impossible to contr easily and is responsible for some amusir effects. One succeeds in adjusting tl temperature suitably at a steady speed on motorway by mixing cold air with tl electric blower. Then you leave the moto way; as you slow down, you lose heate air without losing cold air, so a wave cold air comes in. Then, as you accelera away down the road, a great wave of h air engulfs you as the revs go up; almost animal trait.

Rear accommodation is strictly occ sional of course; but as a two-seater t Porsche is very practical. The boot deeper than its shallow-look appears; tv people can stow all they need for Continental trip in the nose. Subtle desig of the lock makes opening the bootlid ve easy, despite the fact that, for obvio reasons it must include a safety seco catch. A somewhat loose-fitting carp covers the battery, jack and the spa

wheel. The bootlid release inside the car was a little stiff however on the test car. If necessary one can treat the space behind the front seats as upholstered luggage accommodation. In front there is a small locker, quite useful, and footwell pockets best used for maps.

A good driving mirror is fitted ahead of the front door. The quartz-iodine Bosch headlamps are very good indeed, giving a most reassuring spread and range of light on full beam without depriving one too badly on dip.

Living with the Carrera

Most of *Autocar*'s staff would be tempted to add, almost involuntarily after that heading, "Can't imagine anything nicer". Assuming you can afford it, the Carrera would be a very welcome companion, provided that you respected it as necessary. Being in group 7, sordid realities like insurance are a matter for discussion be-

Signwriting on the side (in three colours to match wheels) is standard solely with this paint finish, called "Grand Prix White". It is not available with other finishes. MYX 4L is the car used to win the first round of the STP Championship for Production Sports-cars at Croft on 11 March (driven by Nick Faure). Only modifications for racing were the fitting of a roll cage inside, an external battery cut-off switch, full safety harness and two new rear tyres. Radio and aerial were left installed. Car was driven to and from the circuit (as, in some opinions, all production sports-car race competing cars ought to be)
Inset: Business-like dashboard is standard 911S

tween the prospective owner and his broker. Most of the extras one would wish for are standard, such as electric windows. The test car came with a Radiomobile cartridge player-cum-wireless with electric aerial (£117), but without a limited slip differential (£94) or an electric sunroof (£178). Delivered in London the Carrera

RS Touring adds up to £6,791.

Being such a clean shape, the car does not get filthy so easily as others do, except in the markedly turbulent area behind the rear spoiler, which becomes very grubby in sharp contrast to the swept lines of road filth on the smooth quarters to each side of the spoiler. Incidentally, it is important to close the engine cover by pushing down on the lip of the spoiler rather than on the back of the cover; it was pointed out to us how previous users, unaware of this, had caused the back of the cover to crack slightly.

The tool kit is excellent; five double open-ended spanners, one double-ended ring, one double-ended screwdriver, pliers, Allen key and a spare belt. Several examples of consideration for the owner are evident in the engine compartment. Metal plates carry various pieces of information, such as tyre pressures, how to check the oil level—which is done with the engine running

PORSCHE CARRERA RS TOURING (2,687 c.c.)

TOTAL AS TESTED ON THE ROAD £7,349.90

ACCELERATION

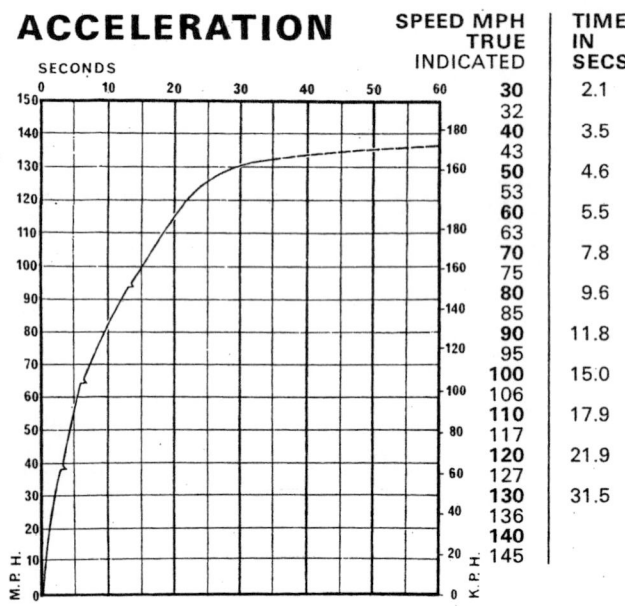

SPEED MPH TRUE	INDICATED	TIME IN SECS
30	32	2.1
40	43	3.5
50	53	4.6
60	63	5.5
70	75	7.8
80	85	9.6
90	95	11.8
100	106	15.0
110	117	17.9
120	127	21.9
130	136	31.5
140	145	

GEAR RATIOS AND TIME IN SEC

mph	Top (3.21)	4th (4.10)	3rd (5.58)	2nd (8.12)
10-30	—	—	—	3.0
20-40	—	—	4.2	2.3
30-50	—	5.6	3.3	2.0
40-60	8.0	5.1	3.0	2.1
50-70	7.8	5.0	3.1	—
60-80	6.7	4.6	3.2	—
70-90	7.8	4.6	3.8	—
80-100	8.3	5.4	—	—
90-110	8.7	6.4	—	—
100-120	9.7	8.1	—	—

Standing ¼-mile
14.1 sec 97 mph
Standing Kilometre
25.4 sec 124 mph
Test distance
1,380 miles
Mileage recorder
2.7 per cent over-reading

PERFORMANCE

MAXIMUM SPEED

Gear	mph	kph	rpm
Top (mean)	149	240	6,200
(best)	149	240	6,200
4th	136	219	7,200
3rd	99	160	7,200
2nd	68	110	7,200
1st	39	63	7,200

BRAKES

FADE
(from 70 mph in neutral)
Pedal load for 0.5g stops in lb

1	45-40	6	40-35
2	45-40	7	40-35
3	40-35	8	40-35
4	40-35	9	40-35
5	40-35	10	40-35

RESPONSE
(from 30 mph in neutral)

Load	g	Distance
20 lb	0.22	137 ft
40 lb	0.42	72 ft
60 lb	0.64	47 ft
80 lb	0.85	35 ft
100 lb	1.03	29.2 ft
Handbrake	0.40	75 ft
Max. Gradient	1 in 3	

CLUTCH

Pedal 30 lb and 5¾ in.

COMPARISONS

MAXIMUM SPEED MPH
Ferrari 365 GTB/4 Daytona . . . (£10,347) 174
Lamborghini Miura P400S . . (No longer available) 172
Aston Martin V8 . . . . (£8,827) 162
De Tomaso Pantera . . . (£6,604) 159
Porsche Carrera RS Touring . . . (£7,193) 149

0-60 MPH, SEC
Ferrari 365 GTB/4 Daytona . . . 5.4
Porsche Carrera RS Touring . 5.5
Aston Martin V8 . . . . 6.0
De Tomaso Pantera 6.2
Lamborghini Miura P400S . . . 6.7

STANDING ¼-MILE, SEC
Ferrari 365 GTB/4 Daytona . . . 13.7
Porsche Carrera RS Touring . 14.1
Aston Martin V8 . . . . 14.1
De Tomaso Pantera 14.4
Lamborghini Miura P400S . . . 14.5

OVERALL MPG
Porsche Carrera RS Touring . 16.7
Lamborghini Miura P400S . . . 13.3
De Tomaso Pantera 13.0
Ferrari 365 GTB/4 Daytona . . . 12.4
Aston Martin V8 . . . . 12.2

GEARING

(with 215/60 VR 15 in. tyres)

Top . . . . 24.06 mph per 1,000 rpm
4th . . . . 18.84 mph per 1,000 rpm
3rd . . . . 13.81 mph per 1,000 rpm
2nd . . . . 9.50 mph per 1,000 rpm
1st . . . . 5.476 mph per 1,000 rpm

CONSUMPTION

FUEL
Fuel injection system incompatible with *Autocar* flowmeter test system

Typical mpg . 17 (16.6 litres/100 km)
Calculated (DIN) mpg (factory figure) 26 (10.8 litres/100 km)
Overall mpg . 16.7 (16.9 litres/100 km)
Grade of fuel
 Normal, 2-star (min. 91 RM)

OIL
Consumption (SAE 30)
 600 miles per pint

TEST CONDITIONS
Weather: Dry. Wind: 8-12 mph.
(No wind for maximum speed runs.)
Temperature: 5 deg. C. (41 deg. F.)
Barometer: 29.2 in. hg. Humidity: 70 per cent.
Surfaces: Dry concrete and asphalt.

WEIGHT:
Kerb Weight 21.4 cwt (2,398 lb—1,088 kg) with oil, water and half full fuel tank).
Distribution, per cent F, 41.2; R, 58.8.
Laden as tested: 23.9 cwt (2,682 lb—1,216 kg).

TURNING CIRCLES:
Between kerbs L, 33 ft 3 in.; R, 33 ft 10 in.
Between walls L, 34 ft 7 in.; R, 35 ft 2 in.
Steering wheel turns, lock to lock 3.2.
Figures taken at 8,900 miles by our own staff at the Motor Industry Research Association proving ground at Nuneaton and on the Continent.

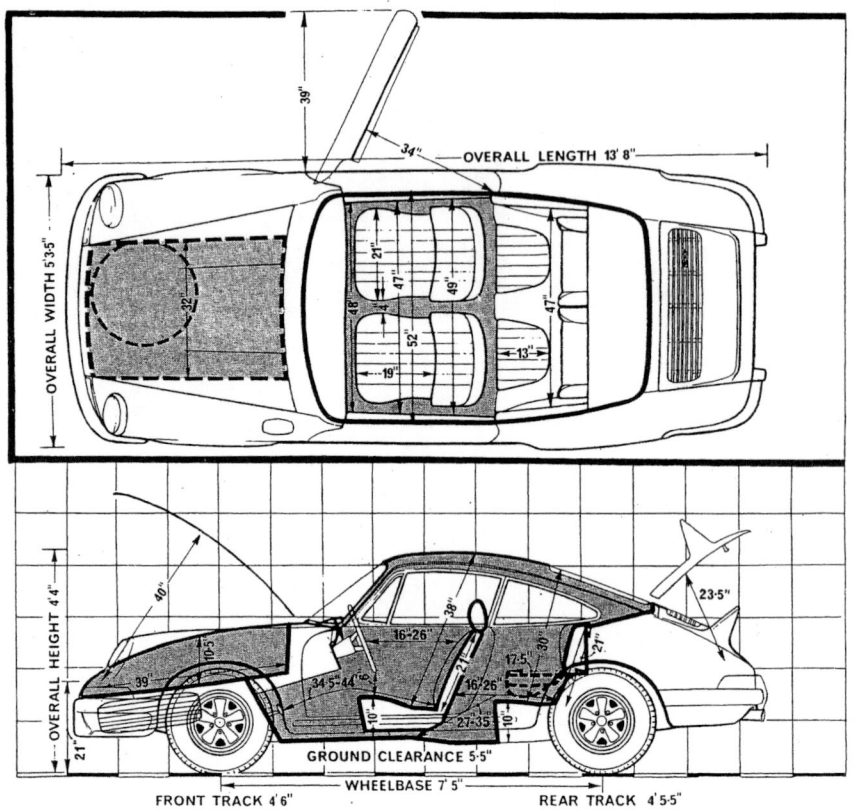

Standard Garage 16 ft × 8 ft 6 in.

SPECIFICATION REAR ENGINE, REAR-WHEEL DRIVE

ENGINE
Cylinders	6, horizontally opposed
Main bearings	8
Cooling system	Ducted air, fan-forced
Bore	90.0 mm (3.54 in.)
Stroke	70.4 mm (2.77 in.)
Displacement	2,687 c.c. (163.9 cu. in.)
Valve gear	Single OHC per bank, finger-type rockers
Compression ratio	8.5-to-1. Min. octane rating: 91 RM
Carburettors	Bosch mechanical fuel injection
Fuel pump	Bosch electric low pressure mechanical high pressure, recirculating system
Oil filter	Purolator full flow
Max. power	210 bhp (DIN) at 6,300 rpm
Max. torque	188 lb ft (DIN) at 5,100 rpm

TRANSMISSION
Clutch type	Fichtel and Sachs, diaphragm spring, single dry plate, 8.9 in. dia.
Gearbox	5-speed all synchromesh
Gear ratios	Top 0.724
	Fourth 0.925
	Third 1.261
	Second 1.834
	First 3.182
	Reverse 3.325
Final drive	Spiral bevel, 4.429-to-1

CHASSIS and BODY
Construction	Integral, with steel body

SUSPENSION
Front	Independent, longitudinal torsion bars, double wishbones, Bilstein telescopic dampers, anti-roll bar
Rear	Independent, transverse torsion bars, semi-trailing arms, Bilstein dampers anti-roll bar

STEERING
Type	ZF rack and pinion
Wheel dia	15.0 in.

BRAKES
Make and type	Dunlop-ATE ventilated discs front and rear, separate handbrake drum in rear discs, no handbrake
Servo	
Dimensions	F 11.1 in. dia
	R 11.4 in. dia
Swept area	F 235. in., R 208 sq. in. Total 443 sq. in. (370 sq. in./ton laden)

WHEELS
Type	Porsche forged aluminium alloy, 5-stud fixing 6 and 7 in. wide rims front and rear
Tyres—make	Pirelli
—type	Cinturato CN36 radial ply tubed
—size	215/60 VR 15 in.

EQUIPMENT
Battery	Two 12 Volt 36 Ah
Alternator	Motorola 64-amp a.c.
Headlamps	Bosch tungsten-halogen 120/110 watt (total)
Reversing lamp	Standard
Electric fuses	21
Screen wipers	3-speed
Screen washer	Standard electric, four-jet
Interior heater	Standard air-blending, type, engine-blower
Heated backlight	Standard two-stage
Safety belts	Standard
Interior trim	Pvc/cloth seats, pvc headlining
Floor covering	Carpet
Jack	Pillar type
Jacking points	One each side under sill
Windscreen	Laminated
Underbody protection	Galvanised main sub frame with pvc underseal and Tectyl treatment

MAINTENANCE
Fuel tank	13.6 Imp. gallons (62 litres)
Oil tank	17.5 pints (10.0 litres) SAE 30. Change oil every 6,000 miles. Change filter every 6,000 miles.
Gearbox and final drive	5.3 pints SAE 90. Change every 12,000 miles
Grease	No points
Valve clearance	Inlet 0.004 in. (hot) Exhaust 0.004 in. (hot)
Contact breaker	0.013 in. gap; 38° deg. dwell
Ignition timing	0° deg. BTDC at 900 rpm 32–38° BTDC (stroboscopic at 6,000 rpm)
Spark plug	Type: Bosch W265P21. Gap 0.022 in.
Compression pressure	Not available from manufacturer
Tyre pressures	F 28.5; R 28.2 psi (all conditions)
Max. payload	700 lb (325 kg)

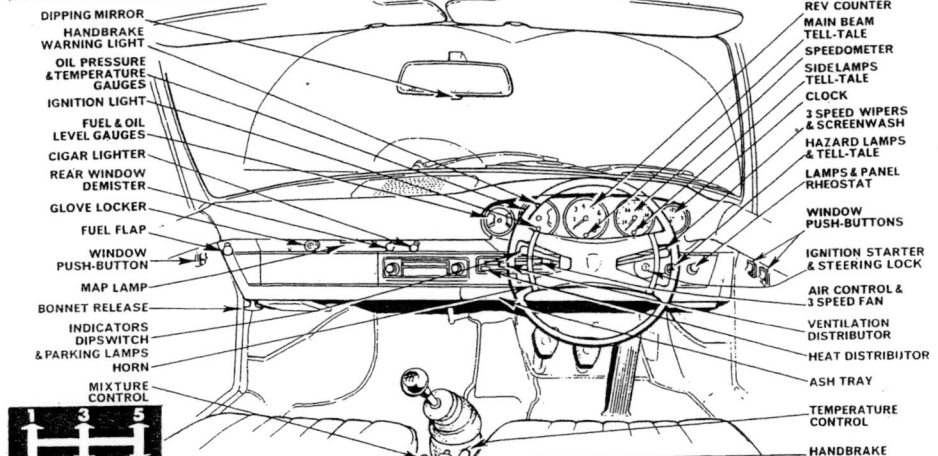

Boot lid is opened by means of the very easily worked safety latch. Luggage space is good for this sort of car. Spare wheel lives under the carpet and is a normal front size. Toolkit is excellent

Service Interval	6,000	12,000
Time allowed	1.90 hours	7.00 hours
Cost @ £2.50 per hour	£4.75	£17.50
Oil	£1.90	£2.80
Oil filter	£2.51	£2.51
Breather filter	—	—
Air filter	—	£2.95
Contact breaker points	—	£0.54
Sparking plugs	—	£13.20
Total cost:	£9.16	£39.50

Routine Replacements	Time	Cost	Spares	TOTAL:
Brake pads	1.00	£2.50	£12.71	£15.21
Exhaust system	0.75	£1.90	£72.61	£74.51
Clutch	3	£7.50	£27.62	£35.12 ex.
Dampers—front pair	1.90	£4.75	£80.90	£84.65
Dampers—rear pair	0.50	£1.25	£37.34	£38.59
Replace drive shaft, (one)	1.00	£2.50	£57.59	£60.09
Generator	0.60	£1.50	£29.59	£31.09 ex.
Starter	0.70	£1.75	£58.09	£59.84

since it is a dry-sump system; what the difference is between maximum and minimum on the dipstick; valve clearance (this is done with a neat diagram); maximum weights and the usual reference numbers.

Once one has learnt what to take notice of and what to ignore, the oil contents gauge is worth having. It does however give a pessimistic view of the oil level, which is best checked with the dipstick. Porsche apparently continue to insist that the owner uses a relatively "straight" engine oil; the car accordingly came to us with a gallon of Shell Rotella oil in the boot, of which its consumption was fairly frugal, depending on how hard one drove.

Accessibility, so far as the average owner will want access to this engine, is reasonably good. The throttle linkage is a somewhat alarming-looking assembly of ball joints and push-pull rods. The distributor is tolerably within reach, the coil is easy, like the oil filter, and oil filling is no bother. As usual, we like the thoughtful provision of a flap to stop petrol pump attendants scratching bodywork round the filler in the left-side front wing. The extensive amount of rubber round the car is welcome too.

Summing up, besides being the fastest of a very fast range of super sports-cars, the Carrera RS is also the easiest Porsche to drive and the most exhilarating. That does not deny the fact that it is a car that needs more care than most high-performance cars; but we think the care would be well worth it. □

MANUFACTURER:
Dr. Ing. H. C. F. Porsche AG, Stuttgart-Zuffenhausen, West Germany.

UK CONCESSIONAIRES:
Porsche Cars Great Britain Ltd., Falcon Works, London Road, Isleworth, Middlesex.

PRICES:
Basic (including Car Tax and Import Duty)	£6,539.00
V.A.T.	£653.90
Total (in GB)	£7,192.90
Seat Belts	(Standard)
Licence	£25.00
Delivery charge (London)	£6.00
Number plates	£9.00
Total on the Road (exc. insurance)	**£7,232.90**
Insurance	Group 7

EXTRAS (inc. PT)
Limited slip	£94.00
Electric sunroof	£220.00
*Radiomobile 108 S/R two speaker and electric aerial	£117.00

*Fitted to test car

Porsche 911T

PORSCHES come in a number of states of tune but only one shape. The 912 is the four-cylinder, 1.6-litre example, the 911s are the six cylinder ones. There are three 911s, the T, the L and the S. They are all 2 litres and, reading upwards, the T is the lowest-priced (£3228), detuned one which was introduced last year. It has plain trim and a 110 bhp (DIN) 125 bhp (SAE) engine. Roughly speaking, DIN corresponds to net bhp, and SAE is a gross figure.

The original 911 is now known as the 911L (£3586). The engine of this one is 130 bhp (DIN) and 148 bhp (SAE). It was introduced in October 1964, 1965 in Britain. Then there is the 160/180 bhp 911S (£4122) which is the real flyer of the bunch with all-singing, all-dancing trim, magnesium wheels à la Bugatti, wood-rimmed steering wheel, you name it, it's got it. So it ought to have at £4122.

All the Porsches have a five-speed, all-synchromesh gearbox as standard in Britain. Sportomatic semi-automatic transmission is available if you discover gearchanging a chore, which is less likely with a Porsche than with almost any other motor car of which I can think. The Sportomatic can be bought with any 911 for £161 and we were spared the trouble of making up our mind about it because the test 911T (T for Touring) had a manual gearbox.

Ever since I first drove a Porsche 1600SC some years ago I have invariably put a Porsche among the exclusive list of The 12 Cars I Would Most Like To Own. But I don't think it would be a 911T. It has all the Porsche virtues. The handling is superlative and it goes without saying it is speedy. The furnishings are something short of luxurious but they are practical, comfortable, and hard-wearing. Finish is impeccable inside and out; the standard of engineering not only *is* good, it looks good too. The Porsche is a beautiful thing to look at, well-proportioned, lean, superbly practical. It is a car that enthusiasts drool over, owners dote upon and bystanders admire. A top speed of nearly 130 mph and a standing quarter mile in 17 sec is enough performance for most people, detail equipment is satisfactory.

It has few of the old Porsche vices. The old oversteer bogey was laid years ago. But it still has an antiquated heating and ventilating system that deposits smeary muck on the insides of the windows. You simply can't see out in rain. Luggage space is adequate but not generous. And there are rushy noises from the air cooled engine at the back. The ride is not very smooth.

The significant thing about the Porsche is not so much that it costs £3228, but that its closest rival costs about £1000 less. Now we know the old argument that a car like this is a sort of investment, it depreciates slowly and lasts longer and all that. It is probably true that Porsches do last longer than most cars. There is ample evidence to indicate this: even the test car had done a bigger mileage than most press demonstrators and it felt, as far as one could tell, just like new. There are lots of old Porsches around to support the idea that lots of people buy them and keep them a long time and if you do this you can probably save yourself a bit of money in the long run.

This is probably why folk buy Volkswagens.

There can't be many other reasons.

But the plain fact is not many people work this way. They reckon on buying a new car which they will keep for two years (about 25,000 miles), maybe more if the value stays up well. But it's not going to give you your thousand quid back. Its long life will benefit the second owner, and the third, and, provided nobody crunches it, probably the fourth and fifth too. But it still costs three and a bit grand.

Even if it *has* won the Monte Carlo Rally.

No, the justification of the Porsche lies less in its life expectancy than in its individuality, its engineering and, simply, in how nice it is to drive. And for that money it has to be pretty exciting.

'A sort of investment'

Fortunately it is. But not in the rorty, head-jerking acceleration, projectile way that some expensive cars are. Porsches are nothing if not subtle: they seduce, not rape. Your initial disappointment at not being hurled into the middle distance, or finding a crisp, short-movement gearshift will slowly disappear as the miles build up. The acceleration is smooth and even all the way up the range, it goes on happening for a long time and *that* is what is so exciting. Familiarity with the gearchange will show that although at first it feels a bit sloppy, it is probably the fastest gearchange you have ever handled. The gate is a funny shape but you can throw your hand from a foot behind the knob as fast as you can manage and snap through from gear to gear at an astonishing speed. It is swift and clash-proof, the ratios are precisely right for a touring car, fourth is near enough direct, and the geared-up fifth hustles the car along at 21 mph per 1000 rpm.

How precise and thorough Porsche are. You feel they know everything in the world about their cars. They even produce accurate graphs of every aspect of the performance in their handbook. Our first attempt to match the figures failed. It was windy so we tried again and they were almost identical. The well run-in test car improved on their maximum speed, but because of rather a lot of town running it returned a poorer fuel consumption. Porsche reckon it ought to come out around 25 mpg; we obtained only 23.

What splendid public relations a handbook like this is. One feels that the car has been designed around the figures, not that the figures are the chance outcome of power, tyre grip and weight.

Porsche handling is not unlike that of an Imp. I mean characteristically, not as a measure of cornering power. In the wet it has a pronounced understeer which will unstick the front wheels if you go into a corner on a trailing throttle. Then you can open up, unwind a fraction of lock, and it is immediately set up on a smooth line with hardly any trace of body roll to gather speed and come out of the bend very quickly indeed. Unless you give it a hard squirt in a lower gear, you hardly ever get wheelspin, the power comes in progressively and seemingly all of it reaches the road. No useless lifting of the inside wheel here. Wet grip is superb with the German Dunlop SPs with which all imported Porsches are shod. They are especially good under braking; you can push the pedal nearly as hard whether the roads are wet or dry. And the brakes are good too.

The Porsche ZF rack-and-pinion steering is positive, sensitive and sensibly high geared. What a pity they have to put a giant steering wheel on; it is the first thing I would change if I had a Porsche as it is quite absurdly large. But it transmits plenty of feel through to the driver to warn him of this engineered-in understeer which counteracts the 60 per cent rearward weight bias, rather in the same way as is done in the Imp except that extreme camber angles are not used on the front wheels. One subterfuge Porsche use is 12 kg of pig iron slung behind the front bumper.

The ride is poor on uneven surfaces. There is a good deal of fore and aft pitching which you can feel through the firm springing, but this never seems to upset the roadholding at any time.

One of the chief shortcomings of the Porsche is noise. On analysis, this is not because of a high decibel level—in fact the noises are not loud. But they are unfamiliar and harsh noises. It might even be that they are noises *some* people like. I didn't like them. They reduced my enjoyment of the car.

The engine is air-cooled by a large fan which is vital to its operation, but this makes a loud rushing noise which increases quite a lot as the revs rise. Also, the absence of a cooling water jacket allows quite a lot of hard mechanical noise to escape and really one sometimes gets the impression that the whole thing is on the point of flying apart. Do not

---

BOUQUETS
- Superb handling and roadholding
- Effortless performance
- Reputation for long life and hard wear
- Splendid gearbox

BRICKBATS
- Noise
- Driving position
- Poor heater arrangements
- Oily demister

misunderstand me. This is noise, not vibration. The engine is extraordinarily smooth. But particularly under hard acceleration quite a lot of noise penetrates the interior. It seems to get left behind at speed but it is quite obtrusive in town or travelling at up to around 50 mph.

Apart from the huge steering wheel the furnishings and fittings of the Porsche are smart and tasteful. The carpet is the woven sort that Continentals seem to like; it is very practical and hard-wearing, but it hardly gives a luxury feel to the interior. The upholstery is leather-like, with perforated panels and reclining seat backs. Drivers of average height will probably feel they are sitting in a bath and have to peep over the rim of that enormous steering wheel. I'm not *that* small but I'm sure from the back it looked like the Porsche was being driven by a dwarf. Porsche (GB) tell me that they have a kit for raising the seat.

I fit most cars pretty well as my dimensions correspond closely to average, yet I never quite got comfortable in the Porsche. There seems some disproportion between reach for the pedals and arm's length from the steering wheel and I never really obtained the right permutation of backrest rake and seat adjustment.

The facia is smartly laid out with clear instruments. The big tachometer is in the middle; it is the principal dial and calibrated differently from the others and it can be read instantly. There is a speedometer, smaller, alongside, a clock and, on the left, a small temperature gauge and a fuel gauge. Full marks to the facia. It is covered in matt black, has a firm crash roll above it, and the only decoration is a strip of brushed stainless steel which is both smart and attractive. There is also a facia compartment of convenient size.

The pedals are slightly offset to the left, to which one soon becomes used. Less satisfactory are gearchange positions which are biased towards the left for a left-hand-drive car. The back seats fold flat for luggage, and with upright backs will take large children or very small adults for short distances.

What a pity Porsches have such rotten heating and ventilation arrangements. It is much the same as Volkswagen's, with the engine cooling air ducted to the interior, and the flow depending on the engine cooling fan. Thus, at speed you get a great rush of hot air, or a medium breeze of cool. When you travel slowly you get very little of either.

The air which does come through the demister inevitably carries some engine dirt, probably a little thin oil mist, and this coats the inside of the windscreen, creating smears and oily reflections at night. Furthermore there are no face level vents which is quite unacceptable nowadays when even the cheapest cars have them. For Porsche money one expects better.

Luggage capacity is adequate, but not generous under the bonnet. For long holidays you would need to use the rear seats which restricts the number of children you can have. One likes the little flap over the petrol filler, but not the way the engine can fluff a plug in heavy traffic. This happened twice, but each time it cleared itself after a couple of bursts to 5500 rpm. The engine is oil-tight and clean, never using any oil in 450 miles. It has a dry-sump and has to be idling when you use the dipstick. There is some upward scatter of light from the VW-style headlights but their beam is good for fairly fast night driving.

I would still like a Porsche. But I feel I would probably get better value for £2782 spent on a 912 than £3228 on the 911T. The smaller car seemed quieter and in many ways nicer. It falls 10 mph short on top speed and takes one second longer to reach 50 mph. I don't like the Bugatti wheels of the more expensive 911S which will clearly be a lot faster than the 911T. Why not a 911T with the plainer (but just as attractive) trim, a little more hush, a higher seat for little fellows like me, a smaller steering wheel, and a 911L engine. At about the same price as the 911T? *That* would be my ideal Porsche.

SPECIFICATION

ENGINE
Six cylinders horizontally opposed; bore and stroke 80 x 66 mm; 1991 cc; compression ratio 8.6:1 two triple-choke downdraught Weber carburetters; max power 110 bhp at 5800 rpm; max torque 131 lb ft at 4200 rpm.

TRANSMISSION
Five speed all-synchromesh gearbox, ratios 3.09, 1.888, 1.318, 1.04, 0.793, final drive 4.428:1; drive shafts double jointed; 21 mph at 1000 rpm in top gear.

RUNNING GEAR
Front suspension independent by telescopic struts and torsion bars; rear suspension independent with trailing arms, adjustable torsion bars and telescopic dampers; ZF rack and pinion steering; disc brakes, 9.25 in diameter at front, 9.57 in diameter at rear with integral handbrake drum; Dunlop 165 HR 15 tyres; pressed steel disc wheels; 5½J-15 rims; 14 gallon fuel tank.

DIMENSIONS
Length 13 ft 8 in; width 5 ft 3¼ in; height 4 ft 3½ in; ground clearance 5½ in; turning circle 31½ ft; weight 20.5 cwt; distribution 40 per cent front 60 per cent rear.

PRICE
£2525 basic, £3228 with tax.

PERFORMANCE

Speeds in Gears (mph)	MPH	Acceleration (sec)
	180	
	170	
	160	
	150	
	140	
	130	
5th (127)	120	
	110	41.8
4th (105)	100	28.6
	90	22.3
3rd (84)	80	17.1
	70	13.1
	60	10.4
2nd (57)	50	7.3
	40	5.7
1st (35)	30	3.3
	20	
	10	

2.7 Porsche 911S

Latest changes to the Porsche range make fast cars faster and less thirsty, and thoroughly roadworthy grand tourers even more so

Porsches have been remarkable road cars for a long time, but none of their 911 model changes has been as remarkable as the transition from the 2·4 to the 2·7-litre range. More power, more torque, better fuel consumption with lower emissions on the cheapest fuel, coupled with an improvement to already good roadworthiness, are the sort of changes that we have a right to expect, but seldom get, in our advanced technological age.

The secret of the increased power and torque is the old one of cubic inches; if you look back to the 1966 introduction of the 911, it gave 130 bhp at 6100 rpm and 130 lb.ft. at 4300 rpm. Scale up from 2- to 2·7-litres and you get 175 bhp and lb.ft. which the current 911S indeed develops at 5800 and 4000 rpm respectively. In practice you never get such straight correlation; you can get the torque increase but not the same power increase as well. That Porsche can achieve it on a lower compression ratio (8·5 against the original 9·0:1) with lead-free fuel and provide better consumptions with US-level exhaust emissions, while all around are suffering worse consumption as they reduce emissions, is a tribute to the combined technical skills of Porsche and Bosch, who make the K-Jetronic fuel injection system used on the 911 and 911S. Despite the high output at 65 bhp/litre the engine has a remarkably flat torque curve and ticks over with a quietness that you would never believe from original 911s. It likes slight manual enrichment for cold starting but the tunnel-mounted lever can be zeroed very quickly.

During the eight years since it first arrived the 911 has put on a little weight—only 1 cwt which covers the extra 2 inches wheelbase, more sound deadening and some mechanical items—but the extra 35 per cent more power and torque renders a mere 5 per cent weight increase negligible. Most of the power/weight increase is reflected in the 0-60 mph time down from 8·3 sec to 6·1 sec which is fast in any company and just a shade faster than the V-12 E in the last issue, although the Jaguar gets ahead beyond that. The 911S reaches 100 mph in 17½ sec; this agrees with Porsche's own figures and they claim 15 sec for the 210 bhp Carrera and 21 sec for the standard 150 bhp 911.

Such figures are fast and predictable; what is less obvious from figures is the feeling of tractability. The S used to be the fastest of the range with a remarkable output per litre from the 2-litre engine, but with so little low speed torque that you had to use the gearbox all the time, delightful though it is. This was still true of the 2·2-litres, and even with the 2·4-litre cars the less peaky 911E was the nicer road car; now however Porsche have reduced their models and made the 911S the middle of their fast/faster/fastest range. Accordingly it can potter around town in 3rd and 4th as would befit a 2·7-litre saloon and accelerate strongly away from 20 mph with no drama, just the usual nasal chatter of a Porsche engine/transmission up to about 1400 rpm.

A comparison of top gear performance of the 2·7-litre S against the 2-litre 911 is meaningless as the gearing is now some 15 per cent higher; in fact the top gear figures are more or less identical while the fourth gear

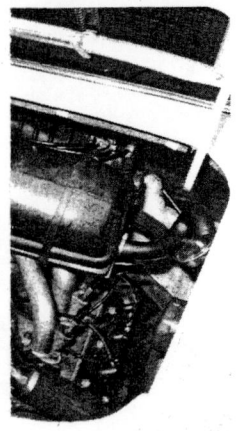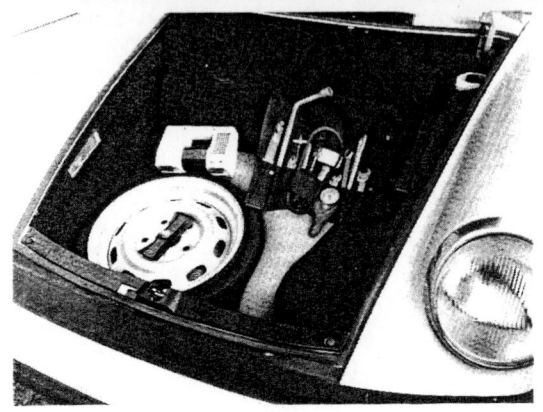

2.7 Porsche 911S...

figures are now much better as the 4-5 gap has been widened to make 5th into a useful high speed overdrive. Porsche obviously acknowledge this by their revision of the gearbox gate to make 5th forward in its own plane. Where before you were always conscious of the pleasant sound of the engine working, it is now almost inaudible until you get beyond 80 mph, and the car is a really relaxed long distance cruiser.

Coupled to the improved cruisability is a greater range to take advantage of it; not only does the tank hold 17½-gallons—enough for a mere 230 miles on a hard driven 2·4-litre S—but the improved efficiency of the fuel injection system makes 20 mpg easily attainable and thus a range of some 350 miles. Our test tenure coincided with the latter end of running in from 1100-1700 miles and we kept to 5,500 rpm and not quite full throttle; even so the car was still very quick and capable of cruising at an easy 100 mph, returning a remarkable 21.3 mpg for town and country use.

Since its inception the 911 engine has used dry sump lubrication with its level indicator on the facia; during our 650 miles we used a pint of Shell Rotella. Since there are 2·86 gallons of oil circulating and helping to cool the air-cooled engine, it is fairly tolerant of the odd two or three pints below the ideal, which is just as well since the filler in the engine compartment requires a funnel for clean pouring—few garages have them available so topping up is best done at home.

As usual the gearbox is a delight to use, encouraging quick, slicy movements of the lever which never beats the synchromesh if you use the full but long clutch travel. The movement required is quite long and tends to dictate the driving position for smaller people; this usually demands slightly bent arms but this is still very comfortable with first class controls. The wash/wipe and light stalks are on the column surround and within easy finger-tip reach and the left hand drops easily on the gear lever. With powerful synchromesh available, heel and toe down changes aren't essential but the brakes are heavy; with ventilated discs all round they run exceptionally cool and dissipate heat rapidly. For fast Porsche motoring this is obviously a good feature, but around town and presumably when cruising at 50 mph only, they require more effort than you expect unless they are warm. From 30 mph with cold brakes, a ½g-stop requires 70 lb., but from 70 mph during a fade test, a ½g-stop only needs 40 lb. At high speed this is less noticeable as the heat input per second is much greater. A full stop at 0·96g from 30 mph with cold brakes needs 140 lb; in fact most Porsche owners will soon get used to this as the driving position makes such effort relatively easy, but it would be worth warning their wives!

When Porsche withdrew from direct racing participation with the 917 and handed over to "private" entrants, they embarked on a rapid development of the 911 not only to maintain its success in GT racing with private owners, but to be well placed for the eventual replacement of sports-racing prototypes by something nearer production. There was a time when Porsche were content to be class-winning underdogs, taking the occasional outright victory on slower circuits, but their domination of the bigger racing category changed all that and the proof of their development success must have been conclusive with two outright victories last year in the sports-prototype category with modified 911 Carreras, the first at Daytona through reliability and the second at the Targa Florio where handling is at a premium. Such racing has considerably improved the road breed and goes some way towards explaining the first-class road manners of the Porsche range.

One is conscious of sitting well forward with a commanding view over the sloping bonnet and the raised wing-tops allow accurate car placing; the steering feels alive, not in kickback which is adequately damped, but in the messages it transmits—you can feel what the front tyres are doing. The suspension gives a good well-damped ride which is rarely pitchy despite the weight distribution; this keeps the wheels firmly on the ground which the 185/70 VR 15 radials hold onto well. On slow tight corners you are more likely to get understeer than the power oversteer which can be produced in the wet by an indiscriminate right foot. Limit cornering at higher speeds will ultimately produce oversteer but most people will stop at the neutral level which is quite fast enough. Porsche have taken advantage of the new extended bumpers mounted on crushable tubes, to blend them into the bodywork as part of an aerodynamic downthrust device; this has improved straight line stability and it needs quite a strong side gust to remind you that the basic layout should be unstable; now it only needs a slight correction.

As ever, the 911 caters for two small beings behind the front seats; with a certain amount of compromise you can squeeze an adult in but its real limit is a pair of 10-year-olds, enough usefully to extend the family man's ownership of a sports car. Most people will keep these seat backs permanently folded for extra luggage space, a worthwhile addition to the shallow front boot. It is however surprising just how much you can get into the boot; using a space-saver tyre, for which an electric pump is provided, allows good boot space and doesn't limit the petrol tank size.

About the only area in which the Porsche falls down on other cars is in its heating. Despite four levers for the system it still needs constant adjustment whenever engine and car speed are varying. Mostly you will be able to find settings that suit for a given journey, but this inevitable by-product of an air-cooled engine with big variations in exhaust energy throughput is the least satisfactory part of the design. On its behalf it warms up very quickly from cold and keeps the side windows as well demisted as the screen. Ventilation slots provide a nice flow of cool air at face level.

A Porsche doesn't suit everyone; some people can never quite come to terms with it—its precise and nervous feel still suggest that it could bite if you didn't treat it with respect in slippery conditions. It is costly too in a country whose currency has slipped against the Mark; £7,000 is a lot of money but a Porsche is the compact embodiment of a lot of engineering skill. It feels solid and repays the enthusiastic driver with endless satisfaction.

Functional facia is a keen driver's delight; column stalks look less substantial than previously but are just as strong. Pedals are nicely spaced for heel and toeing

AUTOMATIC EGO TRIP

The 911 S 2.7 Targa might possibly be the best-ever all-around Porsche.

In the case of Porsche drivers, the word fan is indeed short for fanatic. For instance: you can be sure of an argument from self-styled old Porsche pros today on whether the latest 911 S really deserves that hallowed initial behind its name.

Don't let the debate bother you.

For anybody who has the big bread, this latest 2.7-liter Porsche is easily their best 911 yet and if it has fewer horses than the previous 2.4 S, it still has more than the old E which is really the model it replaces. As before there are three road-going Porsches, the 911, 911 S and 911 Carrera, the first two available on common American roads thanks to the wonders of Bosch K-Jetronic.

Our Porsche for appraisal abroad was most of the better things you can order. It was a Targa to begin with, an S of course and one graced with the semi-automatic Sportomatic system to boot.

If that seems to mean grandpa's go-kart, be advised that the latest S will do an honest 140 mph in top gear, do 0-60 in less than 9 seconds (despite that torque converter) and still return an overall 17 mpg when cruised at pre-Arabian speeds.

We found the best cruising compromise to be a loose-gaited 125 mph which the car would hold at nearly 1000 revs below its relatively modest red line. Porsche fits a cut-out supposedly set for 6500 (they vary somewhat) and even this most elastic of all Porsches doesn't really pull hard below 4000. That's plenty of range, really.

With two-pedal Sportomatic you have four speeds rather like the top end of their five-speed box plus a torque converter and a sensor in the shift knob to declutch on touch. After some years of refinement, this works so well you have instant shifts almost all the time and can still brush it lightly without disconnecting wheels from engine.

Basically, you consider second the midtown ratio, good to nearly 75, third the freeway range with passing potential, and fourth an empty-road gear. First gear is only needed for towing a two-horse trailer over the Rockies. Sure, it gives the hottest starts but Porsche frowns on regular use, and you get hot oil smells at the drag strip.

Actually, their 2.4 engine wasn't at all

The '74 look with text down the side and impact bumpers for a decade-old shape which holds up well.

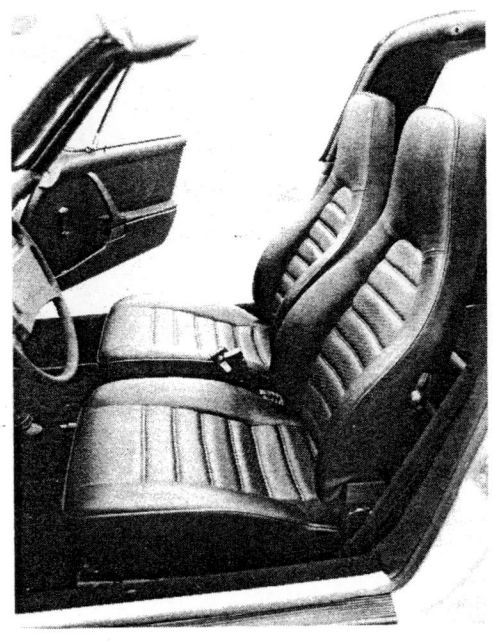

New seats do their best to make rear visibility impossible—otherwise are better than Porsche-ever. Door catches in handle/bin unit are hard to find quickly.

You might find red background for the Porsche name garish (U.S. head of styling now) but bumpers are well blended. Rear wiper is stock.

Extended nose for the bumpers is better integrated than on many models.

For U.S. they fit "shock absorbers" behind the new bumpers. Rival stylists praise the accordian pleats.

bad with this quasi-clutchless system but another 10% worth of capacity is more than that much better. Elastic power is the new S selling point.

Yet this power requires a very reasonable amount of regular fuel and only about one quart of oil per thousand miles.

The chief fly in their engine soup is a still-raucous note if you are not pro-Porsche. Even if you are, and willing to overlook the engine, there is too much ripple and flap about their soft Targa top. Above 100 mph it makes radio listening impossible, no matter how often Porsche insists that the material will stay taut.

Noise aside, the car is so stable at speed

that you are hardly aware of the mile-eating pace, particularly since they have a big 21 gallon tank allowing long runs between stations. This comes from using an inflatable spare though no one has explained what you do with the full-size road wheel after a wet-night flat.

General stability and brake potential are so good the car is even safe at 125 cruising speeds but you soon wish for slightly less direct steering since every ripple moves the wheel. If you can remember that it isn't really dangerous and leave the small corrections alone, all will go well.

Porsche intentionally "softened" the new S as a mid-range machine which means a little more lean in the bends and marginally less adhesion at the limits—except that these come so high, only a skid-pad tester would note the difference.

You can, in fact, order stiffer roll bars but they would be foolish. As is, the S keeps its wheels down on unpaved roads at normal brisk speeds and still hangs onto pavement like a leech.

The new bumpers are about all that has been basically changed on a decade-old body and even rival designers admit these were well applied.

Otherwise, the car remains a two-seater (or two plus pretzel if you try a couple of hours with a trio of adults aboard). But it's a two-seater with plenty of comfort for the main passengers and adequate trunk for their rich-boy luggage as well. It is hard to imagine why Porsche bothers with a platform behind the front seats which ostensibly converts to two seats. All it really does is squeak with the seat backs up.

Pressured by U.S. rules, Porsche naturally had to fit tombstone seat backs which bring still-better seating and lateral support but detract from safety by blocking vision.

Small items are truly polished however: you get four windshield washer jets which work at any speed. You have a rear window wiper. And the dials are all within easy view and eminently readable. Naturally the tach is largest and most central.

Chief complaint would still have to be a heater so tied to engine revs that it soon becomes automatic to adjust its lever with every shift.

And we can always wish that Porsche would devise some way of fitting enough lights to their standard nose. Low beams are only up to about half the car's speed, highs seldom useable these days. Tall drivers complain of thin thigh clearance too.

Such points apart, it is hard not to like the Porsche 2.7, particularly with its clean-air S engine working hard but obviously well within its limits. Sure, this is no machine for the family man with a one-car garage—but Porsche never meant it to be. It's a prime ego trip and easily the finest second car around.

Put another way: a 911 S 2.7 Targa could very nearly be the best all-around Porsche built to date. ●

Familiar 911 dash with tach, the largest and most central item, only clock and liquid levels partly hidden by wheel. Horn contacts at ends of hub are too easy to hit in a U-turn.

Rear is really more for storage than seating.

K-Jetronic is the name of the game—and it works for low consumption of regular, good clean pickup.

Familiar trunk size—enough for two as their tool and oddities kit shows. Rug vaguely cut to fit.

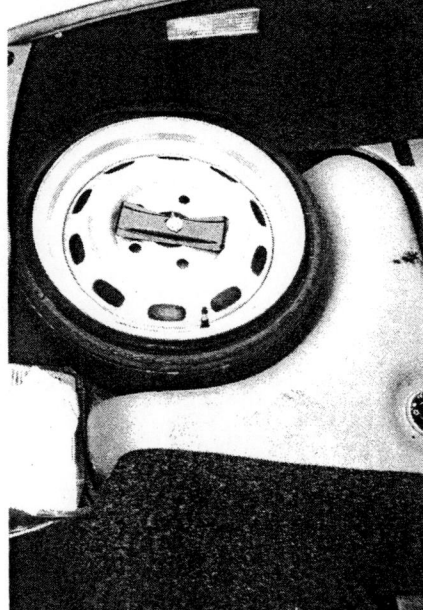

Inflatable spare allows 21 gallon tank.

PORSCHE 911E

Michael Brisby takes a look at the Everyday Supercar that puts all the fun back into driving.

I seem to have been suffering from a mental blackout where Porsches are concerned — everybody and his uncle told me how wonderful they were, I admired their engineering

PRACTICAL CLASSIC'S SALON FEATURE

and competition achievements, but somehow I never felt a burning desire to try one. However, so many fellow admirers of fast cars hinted that there must be something wrong with me when I admitted my lack of Porsche experience that I recently decided to do my duty and find out first hand what motoring Porsche style is all about.

How do you get to drive a Porsche when you have no money to buy one? Quite simple, you become the editor of a motoring magazine and plead with a kind-hearted dealer. Bill Clouston of Langland Motors not only sells

PORSCHE 911E

Technical Data

Engine: 6-cylinder horizontally opposed. Bore 84mm, Stroke 70.4mm. Capacity 2,341c.c., Valve gear - two valves per cylinder operated by single overhead camshaft per bank. Compression ratio 8:1, Crankshaft - forged steel supported by seven main bearings. Cooling — air cooled with ducted fan assistance. Lubrication — dry sump. Bosch fuel injection. Power output 165 b.h.p. (DIN) at 6,200 r.p.m. Max permitted revs 6,500 to 7,000 r.p.m.

Transmission: Tansaxle ahead of engine. Five speed with floor mounted lever. Fifth offset. 21 m.p.h. per 1000 r.p.m. in fifth.

Chassis: Unitary construction in steel.

Suspension: McPherson Strut with torsion bars at front, semi trailing arms with torsion bars at rear.

Steering: ZF rack and pinion, 3.1 turns lock to lock.

Brakes: Discs front and rear, handbrake operating on separate drums.

Dimensions: Weight approximately 21 cwt. Wheelbase 7 feet 5.3 ins. Length 13 feet 8 ins. Width 5 feet 3.4 ins. Height 4 feet 4 ins.

Performance: Fuel consumption 22 m.p.g. normal road use (2-star). Maximum around 135 m.p.h. 0-60 m.p.h. 7 secs, 0-100 m.p.h. approx. 20 secs.

The editor lost in thought having just found out about acceleration! You don't have to risk back injury to get in — access is good.

used Porsches, but he is also a great enthusiast and very kindly provided me with the keys to a 1973 Porsche 911E with instructions to go out and enjoy myself. No warnings, no restrictions and no cockpit drill — the car was mine for the day.

Only a fool would jump into a high performance car in the heart of Kensington and make off as if there was no tomorrow — do that sort of thing with something like a 911E and there will be no tomorrow!

The simple no-nonsense interior sums up the car — well designed and engineered and without frills. The seats look uninviting but are very good, the instrumentation is very clear but the pedals are off-set to the centre of the car and some of the switchgear needs learning.

The first step is to find out where everything is and run through a check not unlike a cockpit drill on a small aircraft. The thing that strikes you as you get into the car is that the interior trim is very plain, the seats look pretty ordinary and it must have been an oversight when they left the headlining white — everything is black, functional and free from styling. If you look around the 911 everything reflects design rather than styling. Those seats which look rather plain and hard turn out to be very good indeed.

The pedals are a bit off-set to the centre of the car and the clutch pedal has a long travel which out of respect to someone else's car I used to the full, and arranged the seat accordingly. The engine started at the first touch and did so throughout the day. While there is a Volkswagen-like whirring (the fan which assists the air cooling is to blame for that) the flat six is *very* smooth. Before moving off there was a brief moment of panic when it became clear that the oil pressure warning light was having a spasm despite the fact that the guage indicated a false alarm — releasing the handbrake put the light out; ingenious.

A Kensington mews is perhaps not the best place to try any car for the first time especially one which you have every reason to believe is very potent, but it really *is* very docile. Both the clutch and the throttle are very progressive and the gearchange seems to be nigh on foolproof even if it does clonk in best VW fashion.

Nobody pretends that the rear seats are perfect. They can be used in an emergency and when not in use fold down to provide a useful load platform.

By the time I reached the main road and satisfied myself that everything was nicely under control, I began using a little more power and when I reached Hyde Park Corner, where there is always a bit of pushing and shoving, it was natural to nip into a gap with just a little *more* power — there was the response I'd been waiting for. At about 3,000 r.p.m. the seat back shoves you hard, all the whirring behind you becomes a grunt and then a steady growl. I think from then on I really felt at home in the car.

Throughout the day I enjoyed that instant response to the throttle and the ease with which the car could be got through traffic without fuss or bother to me or other road users. At low revs the car shows no sign of fussiness and when the occasion arises you can whistle off up the road while everyone is still thinking. I do not mean to suggest that a Porsche is the car for cowboys — on a wet day

An engine bay with everything. The 911E has an air-cooled flat six engine of 2.4 litres producing 165 b.h.p. without any apparent effort. The fuel injection unit is top left of the engine bay while the filler for the dry sump lubrication is on the right above the oil filter.

in city traffic a certain amount of care would be essential — but that response and the way the car slots into gaps makes city driving unexpectedly untiring. The car shows no temperament at all.

Considering that most cars with disc brakes have servo assistance it is not surprising that the brake pedal on this 1973 911 needed a firm push, but it was something that I quickly got used to and later welcomed. In fact, the brakes are very impressive and are backed up by an exceptionally good handbrake.

Getting out of London and becoming more and more at home with the car I began to look forward to finding a few lanes to see how well I coped with the car and how much of the performance was usable. I can see no point in taking a car like the Porsche and blasting off down the nearest stretch of motorway because with a car that should do a little over 135 m.p.h. about all you are going to learn is how alert the police are. Country lanes are a bit more demanding on car and driver.

There have always been people who have got hot and bothered about Porsche sticking the engine behind the rear axle centre line and making the things go like hell, winning races and rallies here, there and everywhere. The

With the Porsche 911E you have the choice — it can be quiet and gentle or it can be loud and brutal. The choice is yours.

PORSCHE 911E

argument is that while such a layout provides the best possible traction the whole lot can come unstuck in a big way when cornering forces overcome wheel grip and the car tries to swap ends.

Ferdinand Porsche was perhaps the most versatile car designer of all time, at least five or six of his designs were quite outstanding and in 1934 he produced the humble Volkswagen Beetle. Porsche designed the VW on strictly utilitarian lines, but he had always shown boundless enthusiasm for producing fast cars and after the war he and a small team used the VW as a starting point for the design of the Porsche 356. This car went into production with 40 b.h.p. in late 1949 and was dropped in 1965 when the SC version was up to 95 b.h.p., so it comes as no surprise to find that as early as 1956 it was realised that the 356 was nearing the end of its practical development life and work began on the 911.

All the experience Porsche had acquired with their competition cars and the 356 were incorporated in the 911 and when it appeared in 1964 it was quite obviously an altogether different and better Porsche despite the fact that the layout and the general shape of the body continued the traditions of the earlier car.

Initially the air cooled horizontally opposed flat six engine in 2-litre form produced about 130 b.h.p. but Porsche have never been content to leave well alone and the present-day versions of the 911 are available with well over twice that output. The car I had was a 1973 2.4-litre version with fuel injection and power is quoted as 165 b.h.p. and has a shade over 21 cwt to pull. A rather potent classic judging by the quoted 0-60 m.p.h. time of around 7 seconds.

Finding out what unleashing that sort of power is like has to be a gradual process so I started out by selecting a nice open corner with plenty of room, out of everybody's way and soon found that the car just went round the corner very flat with a very modest degree of understeer. Braking hard on the entry the brakes which had at first seemed heavy felt just right — very powerful and with a firm pedal that allowed the braking to be graded nicely. Two or three runs just high-lighted the fact that the Porsche was capable of going through that corner a lot faster than I wished to go with somebody else's car, without any trouble at all.

I went into narrow lanes and the car really came into its own. The traction out of corners is quite remarkable and the noise as the revs rise from about 3,000 round to 5,000 r.p.m. is terrific. The gearchange is very quick up or down and the brakes get the speed off very quickly indeed. The car is so quiet on the approach to corners with everything shut

In addition to electric windows the 911E had an electric sunshine roof which caused remarkably few draughts.

down that I was glad of the air-horns a previous owner had fitted just to warn everyone you were on your way. With such acceleration and braking there is no great need to rush corners and take any kind of risk. The best comment I can make is that this very ordinary 71,000 miles old Porsche is the fastest, most manageable car, I have ever tried hurrying on country roads.

I have no idea what the car's limits are, it just went where I pointed it as fast as I thought was safe for my abilities and road conditions, and did it in such a way that I was able to enjoy every mile without ever feeling I had overdone things and the car was in charge. Shown the respect that any high performance car deserves this Porsche is a very safe motor car and the most striking thing about it is that it will mutter along or give you all the blood and thunder just whenever you feel like it. A remarkable car, a car for drivers.